ELYSSE

CANADIAN
Poetry

Von Der Alps Publishing Corporation

CANADIAN Poetry

by Elysse Poetis™
poet

Elizabeth A. Jordao
editor

Copyright and Intellectual/Creative Property of the author/poetess, Elysse Poetis™ starting with © 2007 and beyond.

First original published in 2010 by
Von Der Alps Publishing Corporation
CANADA
www.vonderalps.com

All rights reserved.

This publication is the original Literary ART of author/artist Elysse Poetis, protected under the Canadian and International copyright agreements. It cannot be reproduced, recorded or transmitted by any means, without permission from the author.
www.elyssepoetis.com

Canadian Cataloguing in Publication Data

ISBN 978-0-9782302-1-0

Printed in USA

To Humanity

Table of Contents

Title	Page
Copyright, etc.	
To Humanity	
Contents	7, 8, 9 10, 11
I Am	13
I Know	14
The Ever Clever Human Race	15
Romantic Play	16, 17
Stay Loved, My Global Friends ...	18
The Youth of Our Planet, Version I	19
Canadian Men	20
Diana's Eyes, The Supernova	21
This Royal Night of Love	22
Your Magic, Sir ...	23, 24
Your ... Feminine Poet	25, 26
GODs Visit to Earth I	27, 28
GODs Visit to Earth II	29, 30, 31
Caesar and Cleopatra	32, 33, 34
Single You, Global Ladies and Gentlemen	34
The Lord of Dark and Lady Light	35, 36
Lovers! Be human Tonight ...	37
I Love You, The Secret Code of the Universe	38
I Turn in Bed, I Cannot Sleep	39
It's Cosmic Everything Around	40
We Move The Cosmic Dust	41
The Human Race Does Blend ...	42
We Are Carriers of Intelligence	43
To All Globals	43
Why Lose Your Mate?	44
Peek-A-Boo! One Button Me—One Button You	45
We Need More Romance on Earth, The Fire to Inspire Love	46
Smart Global Men, Kings of Cosmic Lights	47, 48
King of Northern Lights	49, 50
Cosmic Muses	51
Forever Loved	52
Eternity is Love	53
Eternity	54
Sir, Madam ...	54
If I Love	55
Where to Love and Why	56, 57

Table of Contents

Young Global Friends 57
I Am an Artist, I Enjoy Applause 58
We Are 59
It is The Universe in Us 60
The World Needs Stimulus 61
Our Global Dance of Trust 62
While GOD Will Spread ITs Wings Fixing Our Global Nest 63
The Youth of Our Planet Version II 64, 65
Our Children 66
You Are The Actors in My Poems 67
Canada my Paradise 68
The Mind & The Body of the Mind (definition) 69
Our Honourable GOD We Need to be Able to Love 70
Evil Does Exist 71, 72
I Will Adore, Provoke, I'll Chase! The Human Race 73
Who Said That Love Was Easy? 73
How To Resist Desire 74
We Need Exotic Love ... And Order! 75
Apropos! What is Reality? 75
Champagne For The Entire Human Race! 76
Eternal Love is The Supreme Desire 77
I Am an Artist ... I Can Cry, Or Laugh, Or Comment 78
My Global Friend and Citizen 79
GOD is One! 79
I Love The Global Stage 80
Waking Up From Our Dream of Human Age 81, 82
How Much More Does One Need to Be Happy? 83
Let's Pray 83
We Cry For Love ... We Suffer Alike 84
I'm Ice! I'm Fire! 85
The Canadian Polar Love Story 86, 87, 88
Consume Some Fire! 89
Our Love For Men 90
GOD Loves ITs Cosmic Human Children 91
I Wanted to Die a Few Times 92, 93
Overly Loved Without Affairs 94
Today I Think of Our Global Issues, I Think Theatrically 95
One GOD—One Throne to Set The Tone For The Entire Human Race 96
Sir ... Madam ... Forgive Me Please 97
Look At Me! 98
Forget The Colour of The Skin, Let's Create New Global Manners ... 99, 100
GOD is Cool 101
Mind Arsenal 101

Table of Contents

Vlad Tepes	102
Evil Deceiver, Beware!	103
Lonely Night	104
I'll Play The Game From Every Site, With You!	105
Dear Extremist	106
Let's Rewrite The Global Protocol	107, 108
The Goddess Love	109, 110
To Be Sensitive	111
When I'll Die	112, 113
Divine Marionettes	114
I'll Tell GOD All About You	115
GOD Loves Comedy	116
The Happy Human Family	117
Stay Nearby, Please Watch Me GOD	118, 119
The Ugly Truth	120, 121
My Dear Child	122
Today's Advanced Men	123
Children's Best nest	124, 125, 126, 127
In The World of Religions	127, 128, 129, 130
GOD Loves The People	130
The Earth is Quiet at Night ...	131
CANADA The Royal Bride of Snow	132
A Great Leader is Great ART Designed by GOD	133
You! Charming Global Men ...	134
Glamour ... Amour ...	135
The Key to LOVE's Own Gate	136
I Forgive You Sir	137
The New Year's Eve	138
Tonight I Cry	139
I Dream of Being Kissed	140
The Heavens Are Watching Us	140
Holy Struggle in The Jungle	141
We Love The Frozen Fire	143
I Love The Way You Hold Me	143
Women From Around The Globe	144, 145
Life's Long Train ...	146
Wedding In The Universe for Valentine	147
Planet EARTH The Shining Galactic Star	148
Silence ...	149
After I Die	150
I Believe I'm Being Loved	151
I Dream of Sleeping Beside You All Life	152
These Days I suffer ... I Dream ...	153

Table of Contents

The Revelation in My Dream	154, 155, 156, 157
Dear Artist	157, 158
Hon. Johann Schmidt, my Mentor	158
Dear Mr. Secretary	159
Dear Tycoon	160
Dear Lawyer, Dr. Fun	161
Dear Publishers	162
Dan	162
Lyrique Lyric	163
Marianne - The Transylvanian Princess vs. Bob - The Anglo-Irish Prince	164, 165, 166, 167, 168
Election	168
In Love With The Politician	169, 170
Young Sir	171
What A Life	172
Clean Your Mind and Clean The Planet - If You Comply, Evil Will Die	173, 174, 175, 176
Mercedes	177, 178
I'm Blind With Love	178
The Next Banquet On Earth	178, 179
This Gold Collar Angel of Love	179, 180, 181, 182
We Are Space Travellers Having Fun	182, 183
London ... England ...	184
I Have A Queen, Queen Elizabeth The II, Queen Of Canada	185
The Honourable Premiers of Ontario Spring 2002 At The Mississauga Convention Centre	186, 187
I Love You, Sir	188
I Do Believe That I Do Hold ... The Pen Of Gold	189
Who Needs A Poetess? Light's Princess Who Dreams Refined Progress	190, 191
It's Valentine At The North Pole	192
I Wish I Had A Hand To Hold	193
I'll Wait For You	193
Only Love Will Vindicate The Hurt	194, 195
Lady Joyce	195
Lady Maxine of Liverpool	196
Okay, Daddy GOD	197
I'll Be Right There, My Sir	198
You Are A Hero, Sir	199, 200
A Friend, A Rose	200
You Can Change The World	201
The Stars Taste The Niagara Wine	202
If We Are Refusing To Embrace The Mind Of GOD	203
The Roll Of GODs Elites In The Destiny Of Our World	204, 205, 206

Table of Contents
ഊര

Om, You Man On Earth	207
Education	208, 209
Young Sir, Mademoiselle, Calculate The Energies!	210
Is This Life Your Masterpiece?	211
Honourable Global Spy, Sir ... Madam ...	212, 213, 214
We'll Exit Finally The Prison Of Concrete	215, 216
At The Galactic Table	217
Evidence Of Evolution	218
What's Up Punk? I'll Tell Ya Chump!	219
Sir, You Are Being Admired Remotely ...	220, 221
At 17, I Took Amazing Risk	222
You The Divine And Evil	223, 224
Planet Earth, The Galactic Beauty	225
My Love For Brampton	226, 227
Sesquicentennial Celebration 1853-2003	228
The Crown vs. My Anemy	229, 230
My Enormous Love For Planet Earth	231
I Love New York	232
Honourable General	233
Toronto The King Of Beauty	234
The Finest Global Future That We Can Share	235
We All Are Children Of One GOD	236
The Divine Goal	237
There Are Things We Do Not Know	238
The Global In Me, Loving Thee	239
I Make Love To An Angel, I'm Losing My Mind ...	240, 241, 242, 243
Unaware, We Kiss All Night ...	244
To You My Love ... And Only You	245, 246
Powerful Minds	247
Jordy, Little Angel	248
Sensibility is a Quality, Up To A Point	249
And So The Cosmic Story Tells That We Humanity ...	
We Are All Children Of One GOD	250
Our Future	251
Love Is	252
Before I Leave I Bow ... To The Noble Human Race	253

Elysse Poetis—Award Winning Canadian Author/Poet
About The Author 254
(Photo: Elysse, August 1997 - City of Brampton, Ontario, CANADA)
Bibliography 255

I AM

I'm young,
I'm old,
I'm ICE!
I'm FIRE!

My wings are made of cosmic gold ...

Is this enough for your desire?

Elysse

I KNOW

I'm used to risk!
I have tasted suspense!
I know the meaning of defense!
I live life's moments through impulse,
I know the rules!

Elysse

THE EVER CLEVER HUMAN RACE

With every magic mask on face
I will adore,
Provoke,
I'll chase!
The ever clever human race ...
For LOVE,
Of course ...

The ring of light is in the mind
The diamond is in the kind
The cosmic fire in the dream
The love on Earth is the supreme
Desire ...

You are the actors in my poems,
The children, lovers, all the stars,
The love,
The peace,
The tears,
The wars ...
You are the cosmic light in need
Of a tomorrow that's lucid,
That's why I write to you today!
To inform you if I may,
That ...
YOU are Forever Loved ...

ROMANTIC PLAY

Consider fiction, what you want ...
Dream of glamour, if elegant ...
Laugh at night, if you desire ...
Play with fire!

Stay in love, if it feels good ...
Share success, if absolute ...
Dance romantic, if you afford ...
Act as Lord!

Strauss' Waltzes is what you'll dance to?
With me?
Oh, Sir ...

The agony of Mozart provokes your deep romance?

American Classics are symbols of triumph?

Pomp and Circumstance are touching you profound?

Bach, Beethoven, Strauss,
Ponchielli, Tchaikovsky, Grieg,
Schubert, Handel, Rossini,
Pachelbel, Delibes,
Bizet ...
All in a virtual concert?

Sir ... I'm impressed!
Sounds perfect!

Sorry, I missed what you just said ...

Aaah ... Tonight, you and I will enjoy
The Four Seasons of Vivaldi?
Combined with Bacardi?

Oh, Sir ... What a phenomenal ploy!

Guantanamera is also your song?
Ha, Ha, Ha ...
Are you sure you belong
To the ages of divine?

Ah, hah!
You also like the Pan Flute ...
Zamfir playing Black Waltz/Valse Noire under the stars?
Just for the two of us?

Sir ...
How can I pass?

Tonight you are,
My classic aged,
My modern fresh, fine glass of wine,
Niagara's own Inniskillin!
Divine incorporated in divine ...

You want to hold me close
To help the magic land?
To tell me little lies?
To watch the stars? The skies?

I'm honoured, Sir ...
Starting tonight, I'll dance with you,
From time ... to time ...

STAY LOVED, MY GLOBAL FRIENDS ...

You, the human race,
The universe of magic in disguise ...
Remember to love tender,
Remember love's harsh price!
Remember! As a human vendor,
There is a tax attached to
The Divine.

Pay all your debts and stay on track
In order to preserve
What's fine.

Embrace the light!
Run from the dark!
Choose life!

You are in bed with The Divine,
My dear human race ...
You are The Bride!

You are The Virgin Princess of The Cosmic Mind!
You are the global life
In charge!

There is no escape for you
From this smart dance
With The Divine.

Your only option is to love!
The cosmic chase.

THE YOUTH OF OUR PLANET
VERSION I

Look at you!
How beautiful you kiss, how beautiful you love,
You Prince of Lakes ... You Princess Dove ...
Caressed by waves of cosmic charm ...
It's true that you need love and calm today!

Wait please!
Tomorrow, the SUN of LOVE will shine again,
It will be peace!
My precious Youngest Global Friends,
Love life! And life will love you back!
Just trust! Have faith in love!

Don't ever ask yourselves:
Should I die? Or ... Shall I be?
You look like cosmic love to me!
Adored by The Divine!

With every step of life on Earth, I'll guide you to remember that
You are the finest pain of hearts!
You are Forever Loved.

Often in secrecy, of course ...
Discretion is a need! ... but not in poetry
Where we manage to divulge "the well hidden reality."
So, please have fun with the mystique of real truth.

Deep from the net of the immense, you know me well ...
... I know you, too ...
Stay well and love THE UNIVERSE—because IT'S YOU.

CANADIAN MEN

You turned our lifes into a land of fantasy,
You turned us into slaves to love and poetry,
You rule over our dreams and nights.

In a sign of honour, we'll fire our poetic gun!
Thank you, our Polar Lords!
For the greatest cosmic fun.

Without you Kings of Northern Lights
The globe would suffer from the famine of lonely nights ...
Without your kiss ... Love would be missed!

Your lips ... Nature's sweetest sips,
Your kiss ... Heavens we will miss,
Your arms around us ... Love's own wire,
When loved by you ... We want to freeze!
The FIRE.

It's night in Earth and once again,
Love wrapped us in its mystic chain,
We'll dream of you ...
Of war ... Of peace ...
Of London ... Toronto ... or Paris ...
Of love, that needs to be sustained ...

Let's hope we'll dream of being kissed ...

And now,
Let us tell you what we'll do:
We'll play the game of Peek-a-Boo!
From every side, with YOU.

DIANA'S EYES
THE SUPERNOVA

Diana,
The glamorous Princess of Wales ...
The creative breathtaking charm that infected the Earth ...
The ultimate cosmic dream ...

This legendary friendly beauty
Was here on Earth, on duty!

Diana,
Humanely ... The Honourable Queen of Hearts ...
The fragile princess adored around the globe.
Cosmically ... A giant queen, a brilliant infinite noble ...

Diana ...
A royal/cosmic divine power,
Part of a universe of secret, a universe she loves to love ...

In exchange for her great act, her grand global debut,
The script she wrote so well,
In her historical effort ... to help her friend, the parallel ...
Diana will be
Forever Loved.

THIS ROYAL NIGHT OF LOVE

Music,
Soft music ...

Violins of silence,
Choirs of peace ...

Silence,
Nothing, but flowers and music of silence,
Nothing, but rhythm ...

Love,
The only temptation
Eroding the mind ...

Security in secret ...
Tranquility ... Divine ...

Fire!
Tonight, you are all mine ...

Moments so tender
Sweet night to remember for life ...
Two minds well organized
Two minds who realized
That love must be tried
In secret ... In silence ...

This royal night ... so elegant ...
Its love ... forever palpitant ...
Floating above the smiles of pleasure ...
In secret ... In silence.

YOUR MAGIC, SIR ...

I've been turning in my bed for a while now, Sir.
I dreamed of you ...
You, the beautiful elegant global man.

What a pleasure!

You appeared in a large remote room Sir
Dressed in a business suit as usual ...

One hand in your pocket ...

Suddenly,
I invaded your world of calm
And ...
I amused you with some indiscretions ...

You smiled!
We did not speak.

I approached you ...
You gently put your arm around me ...

With a synchronized lift of an eyebrow, we agreed to dance.

We moved in a slow motion, guided by elegance alone ...
I was mesmerized by the palpitations of your love, Sir.
Your lips tasted like love ...

I was wearing very little besides my INTUITION perfume.
No shoes ... almost nude in your arms ...

Nothing to care about in the entire world!
Except ...
Your magic, Sir ...

I was in love ...

In love with you,
The beautiful elegant global man.

And that's the truth and nothing but the truth! Sir,
So help me GOD.

And it wasn't even night when I dreamed ...
It was this morning, here on Earth.

You can subpoena the Sun, Sir ...
It is, my only witness.

YOUR ...
FEMININE POET

I know how much you love to love ...
I know how much you dream of love!
I know your hearts of gold ...

I know your global tactic!
Your powers of mantic!
Your muscle of fire!
Your nerve of desire!
Your tears of regret ...

That's why I was designed to be, your ...
Feminine poet.

Please, breathe!
Remember that,
I am the artist!
Secretly in charge
With the poetic nature
Of your cosmic fire.

You're also artists!
Plugged to act!

You wrote yourselves these magic roles
In order to seduce, attract,
The silhouettes, the cosmic dolls
You cannot help,
But dream to love ...

You are lead artists in this game! The game of Peek-a-Boo.

You're lovers!
Slaves to human kind!

You have no clue
What else you possibly could do
In order to upgrade in love,
The fellow global mind.

Oh, oh ...
How difficult it is!

Psst!
Just between us:
Is it the WAR?
Is it the PEACE?
What do you miss tonight?

Dream smart my Global Gentlemen ...
... I know you are bright.

GODs VISIT TO EARTH
I

Subject: One day soon, GOD will visit our globe.
And ... I believe that my dream needs to be properly arranged,
According to the new global civilization.

You see, the past was pulled from every file!
It is the fresh civilization
That is in charge right now, and for a while,
Until The COSMOS with a smile
Will decide ... if "this new pile"
Makes the party of convention.

And here ... please! I'd like to mention
That the game was well designed,
Programmed to play for quite a while
Under GODs protective eye.

Please NOTE!
Cosmically there is no such thing as emergency or snap election.

You human buoyant Seraphim ...
Save your heavy duty dream
For another age of inspiration!

When face to face with The Sublime
You will be asked,
What is today?
Pssst!
I'll tell you here what to say,
Your answer:
Today is a new day! A time to love aggressive!

That's why, my dear Global Friend,
STOP the outdated human dream!

Please!

Dream progressive!

We can't afford stagnation!
Our minds are starving for progress,
For peace ...
For a simple or a complex good life ...

For LOVE ...

Tell me!
Am I wrong in my dream?

GODs VISIT TO EARTH
II

I need a plan. A modern balanced plan.

I need to find a great JAZZ band,
To celebrate GODs visit,
'Cause I'm here in command!

Let's see!
What else could I do?

I could find a splendid flute,
A little John to pay salute,
A Chelsea with her hair in waves
Could impress and could amaze!
The King of Skies,
I dream ...

Bill himself could play the Sax!
Celine Dion could sing for Him!
Embraced with every magic dream
Globals could happily dance,
I dream ...

Prince William could shake His hand!
The First Twins could ask,
What brand of perfume is that? ... on Him ...
I dream ...

Her Majesty, the famous queen,
Dressed vivid for The Supreme,
Could deliver the welcome speech ...

The globe could be host to angels,
Without worries of the dangers!
Just elegance ...
Peace ...
And dream ...
Embraced by a future well deserved,
Under the universal kingship
Of The Sublime ...
I dream ...

That day,
The Honorable GOD of Peace
Could deliver every piece,
Every cosmic puzzle!
Of course, the ones we miss.

In the effort of growing smart, we need to dream!

I dare to imagine theatrically a day
When all the smart that walk the Earth
Will invite GOD to their lands
Showing Him the place of birth
From where the strongest human minds
Grew with cosmic thirst,
I dream ...

But now, just imagine ...
On Larry King at nine o'clock,
Suddenly!
... a magic knock ...

GOD interrupting his show, as He does, as we all know,
When He wants to intervene.

Look!
The cover of *TIME Magazine* profiling the divine image!
Right there, Dolly with her cleavage
Holding a plaque in her hand, declares:
Wow! And here is a new commandment!
Folks! We need global agreement.

Imagine that!
My Global Friends.

The day humanity will adopt peace,
GOD could be pleased ...
The children happy ...
Seniors smiling ...
Kings complying ...
The youth dancing ...
The responsible adults processing
The dream ...

That day the total refined love could be released
To the entire human race!
In dream ...

And finally, we could see the face of our GOD
In our newly discovered refined dream ...

Dear Global Sir, Madam,
Let's use the finest global moments
Dancing fluid ...
In smart dreams.

CAESAR AND CLEOPATRA

Powerful robe ...
Lose it, Sir!

Tall glasses ...
Fill them with passion!

Soft bed ...
Dress it in Egyptian fashions!

With the first Canadian royal yacht, Sir,
I'll be right there!
My Honourable Target ...
You, king of the world ...

Wait for me behind your sword!
Sir!
I know, you do afford
The game of love ...

Kiss me when the Moon will hide,
Hold me! Sir ...
Caress my mind,
Adore me all ...

Forget the Roman protocol!
Tonight is nothing to explore, but love ...

My lips are yours to kiss all night,
My body idol to your eyes,
The fire yours! My king, the wise,
Until the Sun of your ardour will rise.

The cosmic cause will be your muse,
By heavens you will be excused
For hunting love between the stars,
For setting fire to them all!

My dear Honourable King,
Tonight, you're Caesar in his prime ...
If I unwrap in front of you,
Please, love me, Sir ...

There is no crime in kissing lips!
In feeling fine ...
In being driven by great desire
In pulsing for love's greatest fire
In melting minds in pleasure's moments
In devouring the torments
Of some seconds, so divine ...

My world needs help, my dear king ...
Alone, I do not have the power.
Some of my people understand ... Few, trust and hope ...
But soon heavens will intervene! I know!
Because now, I do have you ... my king ...

My people need me!
I cannot fail them!
That's why, my Honourable King,
I used my crown, love, and perfumes,
To get to you ...

You have the great power that could help my human cause!
In this moment in time, you have the world by the tail!
You are The Global King ...

Dear king, King of The World, Caesar ...
I offer you the trust of my mind and my entire being ...
Let's become one.
You and I,
Legendary power and love.

SINGLE YOU
GLOBAL LADIES AND GENTLEMEN

Single and lost ...
Bitten by evil, mistakes, pain, heat, frost ...

You silly, silly Cosmic Doll ...
It's time to love!
Time to stand tall!

Go look for romance!
Get out!
Have a coffee!
A walk,
Go dance!

Have fun in this game of Peek-a-Boo!

You're right!
Me too!

Everyone!
Let's stop the nonsense!
Let's stop the shivers!
Let's be receivers
Of love.

THE LORD OF DARK AND LADY LIGHT

In the beginning there was DARK ...
Then, LIGHT took charge of night!
Then, DARK again embraced the LIGHT,
Rolling in delight ...

And now ...
The Lord of DARK and Lady LIGHT
Are dancing hand in hand,
Half the time, each in command.

How funny they behave!
One wants fanfare,
One violin,
One wants fun,
One discipline,
One education,
One complication.
One child!
Three children!
Four children?

Two is enough!
Please! Stay compliant,
Life is a giant.

Half and half
Should be enough!
It's all we can afford,
We need some comfort!

Oh ... Oh ...

When DARK and LIGHT release the stress
The planet shakes!
But humans ... are impressed!

When Lady LIGHT enters the room,
Her presence means profit.

When Lord of DARK charms all the guests,
They follow his EXIT,
For dreams ...
For love ...

How sweet!

And so ...
The DARK and The LIGHT forever will rule together
As ONE.

LOVERS! BE HUMAN TONIGHT ...

Think of global romance ...
Think in honourable terms ...

Call your love!
Blend your love!
Be ONE.

You'll love it!

Together ...
Stretched in fine dreams
Silence your minds ...

Listen to J. S. Bach and/or Vivaldi ...

Be exceptionally sensitive to the cosmic pulse.
Play with its rhythm!

Create a special moment ...
A moment that will mesmerize the stars!
A moment that will trigger a higher state of reality!
A moment that will deliver love's great fire in conclusion.

Ultimately,
Be faithful to the rhythm ...

Lovers!
In everything you do, be organized and kind.
Be human.
Maintain a healthy wonder world across your minds.

I LOVE YOU, THE SECRET CODE OF THE UNIVERSE

The deeper the dark ... the brighter the light ...
The finer the wine ... the slicker the mind ...
The lonelier the soul ... the heavier ardour ...
Ugly define—Beauty divine
Forever at war
The Light and The Dark
For perfection in all.

The Light is The LIFE!
The Dark is The FILTER!
LOVE lives in Light!
PAIN lives in Dark!
We are the brave actors
In the play of It All.

Let's reveal the cosmic history!
Embrace and enjoy
The clouds of mystery
The heavenly ploy
The unknown, the mystic
The love, the intrigue
Of
It All.

If LOVE and DRAMA holds us tight
Through futures shades, let's keep in mind,
Being FOREVER LOVED
It is the super-true!
Let's all hold hands around the globe,
And sing together ... I Love You.

I TURN IN BED, I CANNOT SLEEP ...

I imagine the Sun as the flower of light on our global table ...
The Moon as the candle in our global hand ...
The wind, the messenger of peace ...
The thunder, the gavel of the Creator ...
The lightning, the whip of the sky ...

It's order in the universe!
And life ...

Like all humans who are committed to the overall greatness
I myself find progress, very seductive.

From my corner in the field
I take the liberty to dream
The world of peace that we could build ...

It's night on Earth ...

The cloud of silence can be felt,
I turn in bed,
I cannot sleep,
My mind is travelling so deep ...

We need the global health
Restored!

One dream ...
That we are being
By the Same GOD
Adored ...

IT'S COSMIC EVERYTHING AROUND

Before our Solar System, was a dream ...
Before Love, the Thrones arrived,
With magic thoughts ...

It's cosmic everything around!
From every creature, every cloud,
The sentiment of living proud
Is screaming loud.

My Beautiful Garden of Love
My Canada ...
In every dream
That is supreme
You share the light with those in need
You help the planet to succeed!
Madam Sublime ...

How many centuries should it take
To clean the atmosphere of wrong?
To put a stop on the head shake,
To write a common song?
To feel, that we belong ...

The wildness in human race
The crippling nature of the wrong
The evil hidden in one's face
Refuse that common song!
Because it does not like the peace,
Or even to submit
Or to belong to the Same GOD!
How wrong.

WE MOVE THE COSMIC DUST

There will be morning and the light
Will petrify another night!

We need intelligence and trust!
We need to stay on top of things!
With every eye of life that blinks
We move the cosmic dust.

The steps are wide!
Forget the X!

The thoughts are all gigantic!

Embraced,
Pacific and Atlantic
Are whispering the common voice
Of humans who have made that choice
To live complex.

The composition of it all,
The argument of creationism,
The size of every star or prism,
The perfect soccer ball
That gives us optimism,
Will never fall!

If we dare to parachute
In fields of passion that commute,
The likelihood of growing smart
Is absolute.

THE HUMAN RACE DOES BLEND

Why would I cry?
When, I've been loved by many spirits on this Earth!
From pets to humans, if I think, all loved me, I know well,
And I do hope that time preserves ... a balanced parallel.

I'm fine today! And so are you
My charming Global Friend.
If not? Then let me hold your hand,
Close your eyes and let's pretend a walk between the stars ...
Or let's get down to walk the Earth,
The fields that you most love.
Why don't we laugh and dream my friend?
The human race does blend.

How wonderful it is to be human!
How divine it is to be loved ...
How intrigue plays all the reasons
Behind the dogmas and beliefs,
In the race for global culture pluralistic
Modified in faith artistic
Who is to prevail?

Clarity is what we need!
The Creator, the Creation,
Universal love for all!
A world of peace! A home to call!
Where every human can be tall
In its nature.
All citizens of the globe—We need each other!
We need global harmony!
Agree?

WE ARE CARRIERS OF INTELLIGENCE

We have the mind of the infinite working within the energies that dominate our biological bodies.

We are carriers of intelligence.

We see beyond this human life,
We hear the universe speak,
We listen and obey its orders.

Like dreams,
Like cosmic weather,
We are the ones that matter!
Designed to bring intrigue to Earth.

How clever!

TO ALL GLOBALS

To all of you around the world,
From CANADA I send you love ...

Make sure you stay out of trouble!
Now, in your global nests go snuggle ...

And love even in sleep, my friends ...
Just love!

Good night, my charming Global Friends ...
Goodbye ...

WHY LOSE YOUR MATE?

To be rigid ... to be frigid ...
Cosmically, is illicit!
Means acting incomplete,
Absorbed by ignorance.

It is the darkest cosmic distance
In which one can stagnate.

My dear friend, please be aware!
Why lose your mate?
When there is LOVE
To share.

PEEK-A-BOO!
ONE BUTTON ME—ONE BUTTON YOU

Life is the game of Peek-a-Boo
In charge with the remote control.
One button ME,
One button YOU,
The evil ready to attack,
The good always on patrol,
One side of the scale in the clouds,
The other on the ground ...

The future of ideals is far,
The infinite controls the bar,
The very low could be the high,
The moment blindly could comply ...

But you know what?

In all that our lives transcend
The universe will be right there!
Its rules forever bend.

Let's all remember love and pain!
Remember past and future!
Remember those that peace will dream,
Those who forced to fight will scream
Hoping to proclaim
The day of peace,
The night of love
And the Divine's complete self right
To be
Forever Loved.

WE NEED MORE ROMANCE ON EARTH
THE FIRE TO INSPIRE LOVE

Curiosity,
Perplexity,
Divinity,
Mischief ...

Alleviation ... big ... or small ...
Belief knocking at the magical door of disbelief ...

My mind,
The magic assembler of the cosmic note,
Perfect for the heart,
Perfect antidote
Against stagnation ...

Oh, oh,
This mind of mine ...

All set to organize,
Fueled to civilize
The world of romance
Here on our globe.

Unaware of who I was, you helped my divine cause!
You, honourable globals,
The sub-poets of my mind ...

SMART GLOBAL MEN
KINGS OF COSMIC LIGHTS

Because you loved me first,
I'll love you back forever.
I'll write you poems for as long as I'll live!

Poems of love ...
... and adoration ...

Nothing would make me happier than to know that, you!
The smart global men, are being desired
By the best women!
Under the global sky.

Let's try!

Without you Kings of Cosmic Lights
The globe would suffer!
From the famine
Of lonely nights ...

Without your kiss
Love would be missed!

I know that your beautiful eye winked at the globe,
Creating reflections in the sky!

Chasing men does have its price in a poetess' paradise ...

May I suggest:
Without protest,
Let's roll the dice!

Reality vs. Fiction in Elysse's Mind—CANADIAN Poetry

Let's start a dream that is supreme,
A dream in which we shall
Love the Global Male Fatale!

Forgive me angels of my heart, for telling ...

The love you display, is the smart!
The perfect high on global chart.

Politicaly,
That can sell!

And that is right!

How much you're being loved ...

You,
The talented leader type,
You, the charming global men ...

"Every man has leadership qualities in its favourite field, doing what he loves."
Elysse

KING OF NORTHERN LIGHTS

Your lips ... nature's sweetest sips,
Your kiss ... heavens I will miss,
Your arms around me ... love's own wire,
When loved by you,
I want to freeze!
The FIRE.

Forever changed my lover man
I'll hold you in my heart's own den,
And in the root of my extremes
I'll build directories of dreams
In which I'm melting in your arms
Burned by the glory of your charms.

Then I'll even file
Your infectious smile!

Your emotions,
Your devotions,
Your entire being I will back up!
Without a gap!

I swear to GOD
I'll never lose what I admire!

It's late ... It's night in Brampton ...
On the radio, guitar sounds of Mr. Clapton ...

Again, I close my eyes ...
I dream of being in your arms
For now ... Forever ...

My beautiful Canadian Man
My love ...
You kissed my lips again ...

Please hold me close ...

Look!
Open your eyes my love!

Let's pose!
For GOD,
For life,
For global heavens ...

Under our divine intent, the caption should contain details
of how in Santa's Land pure love prevails ...

My gracious, glamorous, extraordinary Canadian Man ...

Tonight ...
Deep in my dreams ...
I'll avalanche with you
Through Northern Polar Snow
Of FIRE.

You are Forever Loved ...

Don't melt!
Just get inspired
And live a life of love.

COSMIC MUSES

They really turned my life into a land of fantasy,
They turned me into a slave to love and poetry,
They rule over my lines!

In my mind I let them shine ...

Secretly,
I do adore them,
And I'm fine
To be the one loved so divine ...

It's like a never ending dream!

Oh Lord!
I should be proud.

I'm floating in a cosmic dream ...

Thank you,
My cosmic friends ...

Muses of inspiration ... and love ...

FOREVER LOVED

It will happen!
I'm just making you aware
Of cosmic changes in the air.

We will continue to be human without so much despair.
Love will prevail!

Purity! Clarity!
Blending knowledge on the globe,
Freedom, peace, love, and hope.

The memory of that Refined FIRE will forever remain
The booster in your cosmic/human mind.
I tell you my Global Friends ... We will be fine!
We are in the process of being big time refined.

That fine FIRE will make us cry ...
We will be washed of all the old,
And cosmic new will take its place!
A new faze in our cosmic/human life
Started to take place.

I am with you in harmony,
I understand the hierarchy,
The change of guard.

In the mean time, our job is to stay loved,
To love others, to be good,
To respect, to live It All.
To shine as humans and remember
That we are part of The Divine! We are Forever Loved.

ETERNITY IS LOVE

Our loved ones ...

The globals ...

Our countries ...
The planet ...
The galaxy ...
The universe (s) ...

The infinite prosperity ...
The love of a human in love with love ...

The pets ...
The flowers ...

The memory of all the ones we miss ...

The simplicity and the complexity of the It All, GOD.

Eternity is Love ...

Love is infinite existence.

Existence is ...
You and I ...

ETERNITY

Eternity, my great romance,
Please love me ...
Give me one more chance
To dance embraced by human passions,
To dress in vails of cosmic fashions,
To see how men around the globe
React to my poetic probe ...

To see the global children saved,
The global streets, in golden paved ...

Then, with a King of Northern Lights
To spend just three more magic nights ...
To dream, to dance, to laugh, to chat,
Before I will return to GOD.

SIR, MADAM ...

Late at night here in Canada
Humans do retire
From life's reality ...

Even from poetry!

We dream with great desire
In beds of snow and fire
About the global love, that we so much admire ...

Good night to you, Royales of Love ...

IF I LOVE

It would be fantasy,
It would be poesy,
Rhythm and melody,
Fire, divinity,
Magnetism, tranquillity,
Power of cosmic LOVE ...

White roses, candles,
Sparkling wine,
He would serve!
Choice? Would be mine ...

Dreams of passion that commute ...
Nudity?
Yes! Absolute!
Strokes of magic and desire,
Flames of cosmic/human fire.

Now, your minds start to enquire
Greater fire!

Just stay with me, my divine dolls ...

Do you know what?
In all those classic protocols
Designed by humans, not by GOD,
Is no such thing as Refined FIRE,
The love that love for love inspire,
So, stay engaged my global dolls.
Go on! Create new protocols!
Eternity, would love to follow ...

WHERE TO LOVE AND WHY

Let me help!
May I suggest?

In Ottawa upon the hill
You'll endure the finest thrill.

In Montreal, the charming city
Right across the Notre Dame
You'll court royally your Madame.

In Toronto, the metropolis,
The great magic can't be missed.

Try Niagara-On-The-Lake
Where the wine and humans make
Perfect love!

Try Waterloo, The Intelligent Region,
On the banks of the Grand River
Where the waters start to shiver!
In love's face.

Anywhere in the universe
Wrapped in my poetic verse
Of refined love.

On any of the continents,
Where you find darling friends.
You can upgrade your global fraction
With a bit of cosmic action
Using the human attraction.

You know that it may result in a mix of ...
Some splendid global DNA?

Remember!
We live in a world of real cosmic dreams ...

To become a global mind
Is the greatest fashion!
Begin today by being kind,
And displaying passion
For:
Love,
Life,
Philanthropy,
Music,
Divinity,
Travelling,
Nurturing children, seniors, pets, nature,
Helping a stranger in desperation,
Reading poetry ...

YOUNG GLOBAL FRIENDS ...

I sense the great themes of your dreams ...
Global peace - Stability
Education - Unity
Progress - Acceptability
Idealism - Naturalism
Prosperous culturalism
Up-to-date safe analysm
In the It All.

I AM AN ARTIST, I ENJOY APPLAUSE

Alone ...
The middle of the night is my stage ...

It's quiet ...
I'll play myself the role of every human,
Even the youthful entity,
In order to touch the cords of reality ...

Hopefully,
From the shades of life I'll hear some applause,
I dream ...

I am an artist!
I enjoy applause!

An honourable clap means YES to me!
A YES means another cosmic/human entity in love ...

Tonight,
It did happen!

Suddenly,
I'm not alone in my dreams!

With a little help from you
And a lot of provocation
From the giant Peek-a-Boo
Now, I find my vocation!
And I even start to see
The traffic of reality
Flowing through my poetry.

WE ARE ...

What a privilege to wake up morning after morning
cheered by the light of a Sun that shines so brilliantly ...

What a privilege to lay in bed at night
and admire a Moon that so romantically provokes us to smile ...

What a privilege to have such magnificent stars
decorating the ceiling of our globe,

Under which we dream,
We kiss,
We hope,
Because we are ...

Breast-fed with cosmic milky smarts by planet Earth,
The most elegant mother in the universe,
We stretch over times
We cry and we laugh
We play and we love
We are ...

We cry when we grief
We dream when we love
We are.

IT IS THE UNIVERSE IN US

It is the universe that speaks,
It is the universe that hears,
It is the universe that sees
Through the human eye, its mirror of life.

It is the universe that embraces us,
It is the universe freezing that fire,
It is the universe's desire
To see us grow in smarts.

The beat of our hearts is the pulse of the universe,
The smile on our faces is the joy of the universe.

The birth of a child is a new homecoming.

The death of a loved one is a return on call.
The voice of GOD does the call ...
The All obey ITs orders.

THE WORLD NEEDS STIMULUS

If in the past the global stage of honour
Was often invaded by fakes,
I feel that in today's process of the new global restoration
Divinely talented minds will perform for humanity.

Every nation has its best!
Search for them!
Please do not rest.
They are The Sacred Global Royalty of our age,
Designed to act on the new stage.

We will celebrate together!
We will dream again!
We will have peace ...
We will have love ...

No evil or hallucinations of darkness!
No suffering.
Just love ...

That's how we have to dream and trust.
Love for the entire human race,
It's the great must.

OUR GLOBAL DANCE OF TRUST

We all need poetry ...
Music ...
Love ...
Divinity ...

Soon, we'll hold hands around the globe and dance
The Dance of Trust.

A clear mirror of a brighter future we need!
I know it will incorporate the PEACE in its By-Law.

The Ultra-New World Order will take place
Adopted with its policy by the entire human race!
Because globals will vote for whatever they love,
For whatever they like, or agree with,
Usually progress!
And order.

My dear Global Friends, I trust that YOU believe like ME
That together WE will be
Forever Loved by GOD.

I'll repeat here again, for those who didn't hear:
I trust the World's Creator
The GOD of our Light,
Father of our Human Race.
GOD promised LIFE!

I'm totally behind our GOD in ITs creative work.
I also know that so are you,
My dear Global Friends.

WHILE GOD WILL SPREAD ITS WINGS FIXING OUR GLOBAL NEST

I give my love and peace to you
In print, my Global Friends ...

Please!
Stay calm regardless of the tensions,
We need galactic extensions!

And trust me please!
GOD needs you too.

For the future IT's preparing
We are living, we are bearing
The chain of pain ...
We cry seeing global young precious life, wasted in vain ...

I tell you friends ...
Just do your best
While GOD will spread ITs wings
Fixing our global nest,
Giving us the proper links
To the future, on request.

I love my GODs intentions!
I trust in ITs perfections!
I dream of going higher!
I love the cosmic fire!
I hope of sharing it with you
In this game of Peek-a-Boo.

As much as a poetess can ... I love you globals ... I really do ...

THE YOUTH OF OUR PLANET
VERSION II

Look at them!
How beautiful they kiss ... How beautiful they love ...
The Prince of Lakes
The Princess Dove
Caressed by waves of cosmic charm ...

Our young need peace, hope, love and calm, today!

I pray that:
Their hands will be held,
Their lips will be kissed,
Their minds will be loved,
Their dreams won't be missed ...

I pray that they will understand that trust
Is a cosmic/human must.

Tomorrow, the SUN of LOVE will shine again for our youth!

My precious youngest Global Friends,
Love life, and life will love you back.
Just trust!

Live happy! Go dance!
Pick some flowers for your friends!
Sing the songs that you most like,
Dance on skates or run the bike,
Drive around your favourite spots,
Play with friends your favourite sports.
Say mercy for the TV! Go watch your favourite comedy!

Don't ever ask yourselves!
Should I die? Or ... shall I be?

You look like cosmic love to me!
Adored by
The Divine.

My charming youngest Global Friends,
I deeply care ...
I love you so ...

Remember friends!
Cosmic finesse
Refined progress
Minds clean and free
Love for mystery.

A rose in your hand
The love of a friend
A mind that will hold
That future of gold.

The future is blooming!
Its tree is in flower!
You're doing the pruning,
You're holding the power.

Forget the dry past!
The future is approaching fast!
Choose to LOVE, and choose to BE,
Choose to accept the mystery
Of life ... Of love ...
You, Prince of Lakes ... You, Princess Dove ...

OUR CHILDREN

Our children will be safe, loved, blessed, promoted.
They are the rulers of the immediate future.
From them will evolve the greatest kings and queens of times!

Let's honour our youth!
Let's feed them intellectually.
Let's create wonderlands for them.
Let's instill love into them.

Let's celebrate their arrival.
Let's dance at their birthdays.
Let's prepare gifts for them.

And, when they love ... Let them love!

Let's create the safest global nests that they need to develop,
Let's give them survival tools,
Space to ask the cosmic questions,
Conditions,
Health provisions,
Schools,
Guidelines in how to prevent tensions.

Music in regards to honour,
Pictures inking every colour
Of one's mind ...

My dear Global Friends,
While it's easy to be kind,
It is incredibly hard work,
And can't be done without full trust in The Divine.

YOU ARE THE ACTORS IN MY POEMS

You are the actors in my poems,
The children, lovers, all the stars,
The love,
The peace,
The tears,
The wars ...

You are the cosmic light in need
Of a tomorrow that's lucid
In every dream ...

And it will happen! I can bid!
I cross my heart!

My beautiful Global Friends ... Look at the sky!
Check all its mirrors!
Then STOP and tell me why we see The Father cry?

Oh, dear friends, we all know why ...

May I exalt you for a moment?
Your GOD The LORD Extravagant
Made you all smart, elegant,
For a future brilliant.

How do I know?
Because the reservoirs well locked
Are being opened for us all!
And everyone will reach their goal!
Loving more! And staying young!
I can vow ...

CANADA MY PARADISE

Canada my paradise
Mesmerized by your blue eyes
I reached the highest state of mind ...

While enrolled in your smart school,
First thing I learned was,
To be kind ...

To use honour as the tool!
To always be positive,
To make life look attractive,
NOT to agree with the word NEVER
To chose the global mind forever
To promote the love it carries
To be there the day it marries
The great light ...

And if ever the dark night
Infiltrates, seeming too scary,
Then to use the double sword!
Fight! Because I can't afford
To lose the love and the peace
That we globals, so much miss ...

Canada, my greatest mother,
Canada, honourable father,
Canada, my sweetest nest,
Canada, you are the best!

I'd like to penetrate your ages, I dream of increasing your pages
Of love ...

**The mind is:
The everything you know,
Everything you imagine,
And/or you are capable of.**
(in the fields of your cosmic reality)

**The body of the mind, the energies,
are also unique to each individual,
special design, part of A & Z of It All**

*Remember!
We are small fractions of the It All.
We are the so called
Children of GOD*

*That's what we are
for as long we are permitted to exist.*

***And yes, if we are smart alive, we are smart dead (so speaking).
Good survivors here?
Good survivors anywhere in the universe,***
(with a body or without a body—in/or any other existence).

OUR HONOURABLE GOD
WE NEED TO BE ABLE TO LOVE

Our Honourable GOD,
Please open our eyes as humanity,
Help us EXIT the monotony
Of this dark global age.

Lift our spirits! Relax our minds ...
Give us opportunity to accept humility,
We need to be able to love ...

We promise that:
From South to North, from East to West,
Our Dear GOD,
We'll do our best.
From hill to hill, from sea to sea,
We'll be the best that we can be ...

We'll love each other, hold hands, dance,
We'll pray to You, we'll take the chance
And risk until we will advance
To the highest cosmic line ...

Today, under Your divine eye, our Honourable GOD,
The global mind began its shine ...

Thank You, our GOD, for our lives, for planet Earth,
For the reasonable global intelligence, for the gift of love ...
Thank You for our precious children, our adorable grandchildren,
Our sensitive parents, our superior grandparents ...
Thank You for all life on Earth ... for our divine pets ...
And thank You for the global angels that live between us.

EVIL DOES EXIST

For those of you who will persist
That ugly evil does not exist,
Let me tell you what I think!
Evil measures every blink
In every eye! In everything!
From Earth, to sky!

My best advice to you my friend is,
Watch your sweetest pie!
Don't fall asleep in spirit
Because the deep looks innocent ...
Remember! That it's all pretend!
The devil is very good at stealing
Your trust, your feeling.

My dear Global Friends,
Remember!
You will be loved forever, just think in terms of global better.
Myself I'm praying everyday, that GOD will lock the devil!
And throw the key away!

However!
I hang on to the idea
Of love between us all
Regardless of the devil
Who in the near future
Will be removed!
Will fall!

Take care, my Cosmic Doll!
Much love to all ...

Sincerely, I care if you can fight! I care about your light,
And I do care about your love for better ...

Oh, friends ...
The love humanity desires
Is: Power! Trust! The Refined Fires!
The dream of cosmic interaction
The hope of infinite attraction
In the It All,

Security in protocol,
And action!

I WILL ADORE, PROVOKE, I'LL CHASE! THE HUMAN RACE

I'm not an occultist,
I'm not an atheist
Nor am I a specialist
In dying souls.

Whatever the sublime in me
The magnetism, affinity,
The aura of the ethers
Printed brightly on my face,
Impressionism or mesmerism,
Godly given pluralism ...

The cosmic magic is my grace,
And helps me to adore, to chase
The ever clever human race ...
For LOVE,
Of course.

**Who said that love was easy?
Romance just a piece of cake?**

**When lips are kissing lazy
Mind's perfect imperfect
Constricts!**

**And lovers lose the intellect ...
And they can become crazy,
Addicts!**

HOW TO RESIST DESIRE

The time has passed,
Engulfed in fire,
We knew that our game it was a must,
To learn the lesson
How to Resist Desire
In our human life
In our work for ourselves,
And GOD.

We did succeed!
We broke apart and free, from all that fire.

Forever friends,
Forever close,
We do continue to respect
The YES
The NOs
The imperfect ...
The innocent in love ...
The fire ... The dream ... The desire,
Life and GOD.

Have fun with life, my Global Friend.
Let's put a motion,
Through devotion, the global love should blend.

Now go ahead and VOTE!
Say YES! Hands up!

Motion passed!
We are Forever Loved!

WE NEED EXOTIC LOVE ...
AND ORDER!

Please say, "It's heaven in our minds, and peace!"

Let's hold hands around the globe.
We need to blend the exotic love with order.

For even better heavens Lady LOVE and King of ORDER
Will be in bed together! ... tonight ...

Through everything that I have wrote,
I sealed the future!
Now, I'll VOTE!
For all the cosmic/human dolls in love,
Designed by GOD
So beautiful and smart ...

APROPOS! WHAT IS REALITY?

Do you know? Do I know?
Who knows?

Ladies and Gentlemen,
Present reality is the poetry of our finest previous dreams!
The never ending It All.

And ... the purity and the divinity of the Refined Fire
In the never expiring cosmic/human mind ...
Part of It All—GOD ...

CHAMPAGNE
FOR THE ENTIRE HUMAN RACE!

Music please!

The Cosmos and The Humans start a new affair!

Please find ARANJUEZ
For instant piercing transcendence around the globe.

In charge with the event,
The exotic singer/dancer,
The sensual J. LOPEZ.

Champagne for the entire human race!

Please!
Make it Niagara!

NIAGARA is the Honeymoon Capital of the World.
Please keep the global atmosphere sparkingly infectious,
FOREVER in LOVE ...

ETERNAL LOVE IS THE SUPREME DESIRE

Lady Humanity and King Cosmos are secretly in love ...
I hear The FIRE chatting with my heart.

I love what I hear! It is phenomenal!
Would you imagine such fantasy,
About to turn reality?

Now let's prepare for the glamorous cosmic wedding!
Imagine Lady Humanity in bed with King Cosmos ...

You see? We didn't wait in vain!

Remember!
We are Lady Humanity, the bride,
So, we will have to find the most beautiful dress,
A dress that would impress The King.
It should be gold!

The flowers must be dipped in passion!

King Cosmos will definitely take care of the honeymoon ...

The bed, will be the dream of dreams!
The love, something I am convinced
We've never heard!

Dear global Friends,
The ring of light is in the mind
The diamond is in the kind
The cosmic fire in the dream
Eternal love is the supreme ... Desire ...

I AM AN ARTIST ...
I CAN CRY, OR LAUGH, OR COMMENT

Buckle up!
I'm gone zap!

I will create a little spark
Of light.

And ... then I'll shower
With some power
Of global love delight.

Now I insist!
Remember please!
I am an artist.

I can cry, or laugh, or comment,
I can scream
Or I can dream
Any moment
In my torment.

MY GLOBAL FRIEND AND CITIZEN

My global friend and citizen,
I am a proud Canadian.

I love the face of our global race!

I cry seeing the vast fragment
Between the some and innocent,
On every earthly continent.

Remember that I'm Santa's neighbour!

And in this life, what I do write is just a dream!
GODs favour!
As a gift for all ITs global children.

Let's savour!

GOD IS ONE!

GOD loves the Earth!
GOD loves the human race!
GOD loves prosperity!
GOD loves sciences, good politics, and art!

GOD loves beauty!
And beauty we are.
GOD loves the honour in humanity.
GOD created us all.

I LOVE THE GLOBAL STAGE

I love the global political stage.
I observe carefully its players.
It is an exhibition of cosmic spirits,
Variety of an infinite sort ...

We all should be committed to this sport!
For better global life,
For a better passport
Towards a better future,
A future we afford.

We want to be embraced by love?
We dream of reaching higher?
We want to do much better?
Oh, let me tell you friends,
Today!
The past was all erased,
By fire!

Let's go ahead without the past!
It is the future that we must
Acquire.

WAKING UP FROM OUR DREAM OF HUMAN AGE

Help us GOD! We need all the help we can get from You,
Our Honourable Heavenly Father. Please equip us with
unlimited, displayable intelligence that works across the fields.
We need human simplicity our GOD. More love for life, perhaps.
More understanding of our human race.
Please, preserve our cosmic grace.

Our Dear GOD ... We trust! We hear! We'll give our life for love!
Our GOD, we understand the deal!
We're Yours, cosmically humil.

We'll integrate! We will get out! We'll love the global stage!
We will encourage everyone
To eliminate the rage
That has plagued humanity, and centuries were lost!
To the sharks of evil thoughts
For a silly cost.

We're not impressed with what we hear,
What we see is shock!
The stage is empty on the block,
There is no cheer ...

Come on actors from everywhere, all humans of this Earth!
To put together a new play
Try the door with every key;
Before we will be asked to pay the final fee.

GOD is in charge with every door,
From every sky or cosmic floor,
With every pain, every ardour that we explore.

One day soon on Earth's great stage,
All of us will feel supreme!
Waking up from our dream
Of human age.

Human ideas? Human customs?
Oh, GOD forbid! Will not succeed!
Who needs the pain of every chain?
We will be pure in our future cosmic dream.

All extremes will die with time! Every nation will be fine!
Everything that seems too strong, will be forced to say good-bye!
That day, Celine with her angelic voice,
Will sing Brahms' Lullaby
To all the cosmic/human babies under the global sky.

The dance of space will melt our minds,
The need for smarts will start its chase,
And love again will be the trace
In memories well set apart for every human coming faze.

Forever bundled in love's layer
We'll sleep tight, wrapped in cosmic prayer.
The dreams will swing us through the nights
Under the sky, under the stars ... Forever!

Global Friends, go on and pray!
Ask GOD for peace! Oh, yes, you may ...
Even for changes in the weather!
For everything you think that matters in how we all obey.

Our Heavenly Father, we pray ... and we pray ...
Our Father Sublime, please help us all dream ...

HOW MUCH MORE DOES ONE NEED TO BE HAPPY?

How much?
When we have the land of cosmic beauty at our feet,
The sound of nature perfectly tuned for comfort,
The sky equipped with the Sun to keep us warm ...
The Moon, to cool us off ...
The stars, to romance us ... to help us wonder ...
Billions of humans on Earth, to turn them into our friends ...

LET'S PRAY

When modest minds think,
It isn't fair!

When worlds of hope all fall apart,
When humans aren't quite as smart
As the heavens once had hoped ...

When death is what they all predict!
Poor humans,
By now all addict
To stagnation and to pain ...

The only way we can recover is:
If we are good!
Go live!
Obey!

And yes,
We have to pray every day to GOD.

WE CRY FOR LOVE ...
WE SUFFER ALIKE

It is beautiful on Earth, my dear Global Friends.
Please turn toward the GOD of peace and progress ...

If we persist,
We can win the war against the evil of poverty!

Remember that we are children of the same Creator!
We look alike ...
We love alike ...
We suffer alike ...
We cry alike ...
We dream alike ...
Our waters drip into each other! Our oceans hold hands!
The Sun is delivering heat equally to all of us, day after day.
The Moon is illuminating our nights.
The stars provoke romance in us!
We cry for love ...

The sky reminds us of the place after this life ...
The Earth is hot or cold with every step ...
There is ICE that has its price!
There is FIRE that requires lots of smarts!

We have no choice but to love each other.
And that's what the Creator wants from us!

I wish you happiness and love,
I wish you trust in GOD and life ...
All I can give you as a gift is my love dreams ...
These dreams of LOVE are ... all I have ...

I'M ICE! I'M FIRE!

I have the ICE and FIRE at my discretion,
So, I will be OK in every moment,
Even if that moment is not OK with me.

I can play It All
I can change It All
I can live It All,
Love and Drama.

An unlimited mind thinks in terms of being fine regardless.

I can be any of the poor or rich,
I can be a peasant,
I can be a queen,
I can be a lamb,
I can be a lion,

I can use the kiss,
I can use the bite.

I'm ICE!

I'm FIRE!

THE CANADIAN POLAR LOVE STORY

At The Great North Pole where I live
My neighbour Santa knows me well,
We love to talk and we believe
That humans on this
"advanced cell"
Need peace!

Between Santa's heart and mine
Now is a feeling of divine ...

Not long ago
There in the snow,
We had a fence of ice built up!
To cover any hope or gap
Of falling into love's own trap,
So, stubbornly we did stand up
To all that crap!

And this cold fence between us
Was mostly to avoid the fuss,
And GOD forbid if any mice
Would dare to think that it was fine
To cross or look for warmth behind
The wall of ice!

Guided by magic Northern Lights
Plus the instinct of my own ... smarts,
One Sunday night I did suspect!
That Santa was an imperfect,
Who hidden there behind the fence
Watched me dance.

Suddenly, a revelation that I shall,
Melt some ice in our wall!
Then maybe I will have the chance
To learn the truth! To see it all.

But when I finished with the melt
There was a hole in Santa's belt!

He screamed in horror! And I felt
His love invading like a beam
Of ice and fire!
Then, I scream!
Filled with desire
When the fence
Came crumbling,
And I fell flat
On top of him!

That's when it happened! Swear to GOD!
The Pole got hotter, and on the spot
We melted inside love's own pot.

Then Santa's arms holding me tight
Drove me insane!
I lost my mind!
What kind of devil? Serafim?
Is this one? To make me fall
In love with him!

A bride on skates when all that fire
From Santa's love melted my roof
Oh! Please believe me! I can prove!
How all my icicles turned to candy, in a poof!

Santa with his toy bag handy,
Stuffed it full, prepared the sled,
All arrangements were made
With the reindeers on hand
And with Rudolf in command,
To spend the honeymoon just sliding
On love's land.

Today we moved into our Polar Ice Castle,
Surrounded by fire
Of love and desire.

Our two polar babies, Polaris and Snow-Dolly
Who play around their father Santa Clause every day,
Can tell you how he always says:
Love is the game of Peek-a-Boo
For mommy, daddy,
You and you,
Let's play!

Stay well, my beautiful Global Friends!
Be good and play like Santa Clause and me,
Like Polaris, our baby boy, and Snow-Dolly, our baby girl..

Love is the game of Peek-a-Boo
For Ice and Fire,
Me and you ...

My charming Global Friends,
Let's play!

CONSUME SOME FIRE!

My Global Friends in love ...
Consume some fire!
Don't starve!

Hold a hand ...
Caress a face ...
Stay in command!
Don't stop the chase
Of life's desire.

All that you need to do is,
Complement!
The FIRE.

OUR LOVE FOR MEN

Our love for MEN will never die!
We'll take the chance under my sky
To never, ever say goodbye!
To their love ...

You MEN!
Our beautiful cosmic stars ...
We'll give our love to you
In times of peace ...
Of wars ...

Our verses mention clear!
The fire that we feel,
The passion you instill
Deep in our hearts ...

Our Charming Global MEN,
Sensitive and well equiped with love
And global smarts ...

GOD LOVES ITS COSMIC/HUMAN CHILDREN

GOD loves you
GOD loves me
GOD loves ITs cosmic/human children
Through each history.

Let's not cry
Why should we die
When we could play
Under the sky.

Let's all dance
Let's take the chance
To jump the magic
Cosmic fence.

Once up there
We can share
The famous cosmic divine flare
Of LOVE.

I WANTED TO DIE A FEW TIMES

As a child,
I was playful and smart,
But as a youth, life turned so hard ...

The mystic high,
I had no sky
To hide below!

I ended up asking myself, "What do I know?"

Being under the microscope
With little hope ...
I nearly died inside!
I nearly lost my fragile pride!

But one day,
Zap!
A magic shower of new power
Came over me, and like a rocket
I stood up!
When from my mind's own pocket
Surfaced a guide,
Encouraging new love and mature pride.

As I was regaining trust
I cleaned my mirror of life's dust
And I looked inside my eyes ...
Where is the Sun on my blue skies?

Oh, dear GOD! Connect my vibes!
Your love for me, is the great must!

Today,
I feel just love! I'm strong!
Because I know! I don't belong
In all that pain, in all that cry
That blocked my vision
Brought confusion
By whispering the ugly thoughts,
"You're not important ... You should die ..."

OVERLY LOVED WITHOUT AFFAIRS

I've been loved from a distance all my life.
Men that could not approach me desired me most.
Whisper after whisper reaffirmed that reality.
The intriguing experiences never stopped.

So, one day I did cry and asked my GOD, "Have I lost at love?"

Before, I felt that the heavens were all mine!
I felt that the essence of all that finesse
In all those men that took the chance
To ask for love ... and listen to my whisper of refuse ...
Was something normal!
I often was amused!

They love me as they should! I am desirable!
Look at them!
How they refine their dreams from a distance ... How they suffer ...

But, secretly ... in my own way, I loved them back for loving me.

Sometimes I thought,
They do not even know me, yet, they will think of me tonight ...
And forever ...
Often I would reassure my mind of that while in front of the mirror
admiring my young, perfect, nude body.

Can you see my Global Friends how the past managed to conceive
the architecture of my future theatrical dreams? That's the reality!
I was designed to feed on dreams!
I AM the poetry.

TODAY
I THINK OF OUR GLOBAL ISSUES,
I THINK THEATRICALLY

I stop and think that rules are made
By strange, entangled in a braid.

Who made the rules
Was too afraid to use the tools!
The sky and sea,
The charm and shade of every tree,
The Sun,
The Moon
And every star
That know how high should be the bar
Of those in love ...

I'll sing the song
"We all belong"
And I will say,
Love is the game of Peek-a-Boo
For him and her,
For me and you ...

Let's play!

ONE GOD—ONE THRONE
TO SET THE TONE FOR THE ENTIRE HUMAN RACE

We need the brave, we need the smart,
We need the graph of every chart of modern needs;
The hearts with most seductive bits.

The youngest of the universe
In love with life they should rehearse
The fancy acts of love on Earth.

And children ... Let's adore them more,
Teach them how to swim ashore
Towards the land of lasting peace
That some, do miss ...

What do we need? What do we need?
In order to advance, succeed.
We need all the extravagant!
The thinking of the elegant!
The spirits waving real flags of smarts and peace!

When globally we will hold hands
And trust each other like good friends
The open heavens will command
Transfer of love in human hand!
We'll feel the fire of the dream
The magic of Divine Sublime
We'll see the globe as Holy Land!
One GOD!
One throne!
To set the tone, for everlasting love and peace in the It All.
Including us all the extraordinary global people.

SIR ... MADAM ... FORGIVE ME PLEASE ...

Under the global stellar sky
I'll be the greatest lady, until the day I'll die ...

It is my feminine finesse that should proclaim
"That silly fame ..."

It's night in Canada, and again
Love wrapped me in its mystic chain,
I'll dream of you ... of war ... or peace ...
Of London ... New York ... or Paris ...
Of love, that needs to be sustained ...

I hope I'll dream of being kissed ...

Good night,
My Kings ...
My Queens ...
My global nocturnal friends ...

LOOK AT ME!

Look at me!

I dare to write
All the wrong
And all the right.

Am I strong?
No friends!
Not quite.

I'm fragile ...

Please don't laugh!
Please don't smile!
'Cause I'm shy ...
And ...
You could make me cry
For a while.

FORGET THE COLOUR OF THE SKIN, LET'S CREATE NEW GLOBAL MANNERS

I care about the globe!
That's why I cry.
I really could just walk away
And say goodbye ...
But I can't!
I can't pretend to be
Blind to misery.

And I know well that I can help
My friends on Earth to come together
And learn to love this life forever
Time after time.

Believe me, please! That love does matter.

Let's all create new global manners,
Forget the colour of the skin!
Or feathers.

Forgive me if I sound tough!
I'm tired of that "evil stuff."
Look at them! They are so glad
To see us running, all in panic,
How satanic!

Catch them all and make them pay
For the dark of every day!

To hell with you!
Tyrants of dark.

We heard your view!
Your evil bark.
You have no fans,
Nor smart defense
In our global modern times,
Or ever!

So many times, it does appear
That history did show us clear
How dark desires and dark fear
Organized by evil mob
Can spread across our smart globe
With no regards for the great soul!
Just dominance as the dark hope!
To tie us up in evil rope.

Remember how in the past
We endured blast after blast?

Remember then the beauty days
And the royal golden trays
Filled with divine?
So long ago when for a while, humanity was doing fine?

But later,
Civilization after civilization
Lost the right to right direction.
Empire after empire
Lost the command, lost the desire
To fight the evil infiltrator
Self-proclaimed "The Light's Dictator"
The shepherd of the silly flock,
The flock that was too deaf to hear the cosmic knock.

GOD IS COOL

The GOD I know
Is really cool.

Regardless what you have to show,
Regardless of your school,
He'll love ya, man!

Talk to GOD in terms of good,
Talk to GOD about your heart,
Talk to GOD about your pain ...
I promise! It won't be in vain.

I know you're smart!
You'll talk to GOD, today.

MIND ARSENAL

Resist!
Please, Sir ... Madam ...
Unless the world is on fire
Unless the devil strikes,
Unless the power start to slip
Down the galactic wire,
Don't strike, my friends,
Resist!

Enjoy your cosmic power!
H's there, mostly dormant.
Until your final day, my friend,
Be noble, elegant.

VLAD TEPES

It is the truth! He spiked them all!
That's what VLAD did to all the bad, the domestic deceivers and
traitors, and the strange invaders, kidnappers, thieves, rapists.

Ones upon a time,
He was a eight year old Wallachian Prince ...
The famous prince you upset, kidnapped,
Who used great fear, your evil trap!

VLAD tricked, burned, spiked you thieves and traitors,
Then turned against the great invaders.

Oh, poor, poor you ...
He spiked your bodies through the neck
And forced you across the Danube back
For good!

You called him Dracul! Meaning Devil.
You'll never be at that man's level!
Even today "his spiky mood"
Is romanticized by Hollywood.

If he was alive, VLAD would revive a hell for all deceivers!
The darkest hole!
Without the rules of protocol,
And he would say:
On our clean and healthy globe
Heavy with love and human hope
Who needs this evil mole?
That dreams control.
Let's spike them all!

EVIL DECEIVER, BEWARE!

You'll come face to face with a VLAD of today.

I tell you,
If alive, VLAD would provoke
Your own devils masked in black
To grab your spirit by the neck
And nail it down to the floor
With no escape from the odor
Of blood and death,
Your special brand
Perfume of horror!

Your trademark,
Sign
Of your satanic honour,
That could be announced
By a cold bell,
In hell!

And VLAD would ask:
Instead of living smart and well,
With friends on Earth ...
You promote hell?

What do you think?

You scam! Remember!
Your last requests, will not be heard!
You don't deserve it from the hurt!
Quite soon, you'll be erased, without a trace
From the cosmic/human face. Forever!

LONELY NIGHT

The weather starts to brush its wind
On the planet this great night ...
Alone again ... I went outside to check for stars
I noticed the sky organized
Ready to bring us global dreams of everlasting love ...

It's warm now on this lonly night ...
A Lady Bug, I will admit,
Is walking over my poems
Playing all the antic games
I will permit.

Another one, quite in gallop
Is running over every proof
Just printed out,
Without a doubt
It is a HE, and did salute.
How cute!

I took the magnifying glass,
I built a bed of fresh, green grass,
To see how they behave in a group,
Now, through the glass I start to snoop
The mini-truth.

I guess, they were in a mood for play!
Now let me tell you, if I may,
How Lady Bug "The Juliet"
Performed a funny pirouette.
Romeo like a small comet
Fell on my palm ... Look at his charm!

I'LL PLAY THE GAME FROM EVERY SITE, WITH YOU!

We all belong to the same GOD,
Remember that!

And now,
Let's chat!

Here in CANADA where I live
I'm facing an affidavit
In which I swear to love forever
To fight for all the rights that matter
To make sure that I excite, all the bright.

But now, before I'll say good night,
Let me tell you what I'll do!
I'll play the game of Peek-a-Boo
From every site,
With you!

Or maybe not.
I'm really sleepy my good friends,
Aaah ... It's 1:00 A.M. at night ...

I'll dream how I should fight
For higher cosmic love ...
It is a kiss that I do miss
Tonight ...
Or an embrace ...

Or maybe, I just need some sleep ...
And peace ...

DEAR EXTREMIST

To be a fanatic of some sort,
Doesn't mean that you are strong.
You are delusional!
Rolling a ball outside the court of fame,
In shame!

The ordinary globals question,
Sometimes they shiver ...
Engulfed in fear, they burn with fever!
At the sound of horror
They put aside the honour,
No longer feeling guilty
They end up asking:
Why are these devils so fanatic?
Why are they on our planet?

I tell you, my Global Friends ...
Nor Atlantic or Pacific
Produce waves so scientific
To crash the icebergs in the way
Of minds of stone, of minds of clay.
But hey! Can you see?
Somehow the horror carries itself along the infinite of the It All.
It's here as we speak today! In our modern 21st Century,
Eh?

Reality?
In a few cases still, primitive attitudes are a problem on our planet,
And that's the truth!

Where did it start? Where will it stop?

LET'S REWRITE THE GLOBAL PROTOCOL

Education can eradicate hate, humanity's greatest enemy.
But for now ...
When we see the discrepancies, the extremes or the miracles ...
How can we not ask?
From where comes the new global smart?
How low are others on life's chart?
Wonder, what "express" does drop
On our Earth the rotten crop?

Evil attacks ladies, gentlemen, sensitive seniors,
Children, pets, the environment ...
Evil is "the rotten crop."

My smart Global Friends,
Do you dream of seeing evil placed in a corner of the planet?
In charge with it, a spooky comet?
Smacked every time it does misbehave?
Zapped with some sissy microwave?
To force it to learn the difference
Between submitting to past-tense
Or to the future in progress?
Do you dream of seeing the bad converted one by one,
From evil, to smart and brave,
For the good of overall?

Good Global Citizens,
Please learn to tolerate
The semi-innocent.
Please love them, with caution though.
Help them see!
And help them grow.

You'll be surprised how some could be
Only temporarily insane.

Here, between you and I,
Let's not remain slaves to life's pain.
Let's redirect love and intellect
For the light ofIt All.

Let's rewrite the global protocol
Of war and peace.

Please include the entire global population
In the book of GODs salvation.

Give them love!
Please give them reason!
To awake for the new season
In the Garden of Divine.

If we are growing smart and kind
My dear Global Friends,
All humans on planet Earth,
Together,
We will be fine.

My dear Global Friends, you who remained humil,
I know the twisted truth you're facing day by day ...
In everything that's false, or real ...

I know all that you see ... I feel all that you feel ...
That's why, my dear friends,
Myself I stay engaged,
Available in the deep spirit of all ...

Oh yes, I can be paged. I'll answer every telepathic question, call,
Big ... Small ... Through poetry ...
My mind is set to work with pleasure, for the It All.

THE GODDESS LOVE

I'd like to see more LOVE on Earth ...
Nothing shines like its bright face!
The fire of its power cannot be replaced.
Its smart vibrations invading every cosmic/human fibre ...

It is its fire that we want to hold,
And that's how we would want to die,
Hostages forever in the arms of Love
On every plane of every sky ...
There is no question why!

My friends in torture,
Let's listen to the cosmic notes!
To music, fiction, anecdotes ...
To laughs of children, to the sea,
To all the written poesy ...
To hearts that beat for love alone,
To those who love without pardon ...
To birds announcing sunny days ...
To youth who for the first time chase
The Goddess Love ...

Let's love completely smart this life,
If parent, child, husband, wife,
Let's find the feelings we acquire ...

Do not forget!
The grandparents also desire That Smart Fire.

It's LOVE, my friends!
For generations
It worked in every aspect.
Needs no translations,

It is the only thing that is perfect
Under the sky.

Why when in love the globals shy,
Like children, all comply?

Regardless of the rules of life ...

Because LOVE is The Light,
It's you ...
It's me ...
It is The Finest Goddess
Of All ETERNITY.

TO BE SENSITIVE

It is a quality ... up to a point.
Sensitivity prolonged, and/or taken to extremes
Can become a liability,
A nightmare!

Without discrimination sensibility can affect:
Any person,
Any nation,
Any galaxy,
Any universe.

Complains stretched over long periods of cosmic time
Can make us look weak,
Even incompetent.

Chronic complains are not part of any modern mind.
Never were!
Will never be!

My Global Friends,
Relax!
Love modernism!

Please,
Let it be.

WHEN I'LL DIE

The King of our Universe, my GOD ...
The GOD I pray,
I trust
And I obey,
The light of every light in memory of human kind
Aligned in every cosmic line of time ...

The GOD of Demi-Gods, I love to love ...
GOD loves me back,
I know!

And I can show how much.

One moment! I need to check and see,
Could eternity be embossed in me
Like poetry?

But being human, first I need a slice of lime
In my sweet cup of earthly tea of Rosemary ...

And now, let's see!
When I will die, I told my dear child
That one thing would be enough
To calm my mind, to help me fly
Towards the stars, far in the sky ...

Before the angels of divine will come to guide me away,
Elizabeth! Please toll the global bell,
Include a note of love from Ordinary People, Pachelbel.

The Sublime will cry that day for humanity ... I know it well ...

Tears will roll out of the blue sky,
The Sun will struggle to stay dry ...

That day, GODs global poetry will freeze in time.

The tears will be for the extraordinary human love
That will be left in print behind
In hopes that humans will be kind ...

The love that in that moment, I'll have to say goodbye
On my way to GOD
For whom I work,
Where I belong,
Until another time ...

DIVINE MARIONETTES

The ones that know ...

The flexible in infinite
The servants of the human race
The ones on pillow next to death
The ones committed to the truth
Those who sustain the cosmic breath
Committed to the overall
Committed to progress ...

They play, they roll, defend the ball,
With guaranteed success.

Sometime they cry along with us,
Sometime they die before
We manage to recognize
What they were crying for.

I'LL TELL GOD ALL ABOUT YOU

I'll tell GOD all about you! About the game of Peek-a-Boo
Santa and the Polar Babies
Global gentlemen and ladies
About the kisses we received
Dreams of the future we conceived
Some leaders we remember well
Like The German Chancellor Merkel,
Kennedys, Bushes and Clintons,
Thatcher, Mitterrand and Regans,
Bezos, Bronson, Weston, Trump, Gates,
Blair, Harper, Arnold of California and Lady Maria,
About The Queen and her Empire,
About the humans that perspire
In their search for wealth and love ...

GOD knows the Holly Pope in Rome
The Rogers Centre called Sky-Dome
The super-scientists on Earth
Our planet's famous birth
The historical profets
Classic musicians and poets ...
GOD knows the real Hollywood
Knows all the good things that could
Evolve on Earth ...
But, I'll tell GOD about the science, space travelling, flying cars,
Quantum, carbon, hydrogen, every train and every plain,
The enormous knowledge we humans managed to gain,
The aquarium built deep in the ocean,
The Space Station that will be The Cosmic Titanic ...
Oh! My dear Global Friends, please, do not panic!
Please relax ... I'll keep some of the human secrets.

GOD LOVES COMEDY

When I'll go home to our heaven,
Oh, my dear Global Friends ...
What do I do?

I think I know!
I'll ask GOD to give me a smart army,
I'd like to take command and come right back!
To build and finish every deck
Needed to reach the sky.

I'll tell you why!

Because we all belong to heavens
Where global comedies have chances!

Here on Earth there are exceptions.
Just in few cases—Errors are made in famous places.
For example, in Toronto at Yuck, Yuck's ...
Just ask Jim Carrey!
You can't duck if you are dressed in too much blue
For Yuck's game of Peek-a-Boo.
Hmmm ... What a loss!
False? Or true?

My dear Global Friends,
You understand ... GOD loves comedy!
Because it is pain's best global remedy.

About the future of comedy?
It will be bright. I know the truth! I heard it clear!
From GOD ... HE whispered gently in my ear.

THE HAPPY HUMAN FAMILY

Life is so beautiful ... My GOD, I thank you so ...
I love so much your opera ... filled with intrigue ...
The sciences of every tone
The queens and kings on every throne
Of war ... Of peace ...

Day and night humans wake up
To high levels of smart light.

Some, refuse the evening nap!
Like the intelligent ones who You made them, GOD,
So sleepless ... so aware, so actively elegant ...

I can see! Minds wearing great human costumes,
Divine perfumes,
Sleek smart fashions, royal hats,
They parade the global pets
And hand in hand daily they walk
Talking every single talk ...
They exist and they persist!
That it can go on in the same fashion.

My Dear GOD,
Strike them with passion!
Invest in them greater ambition,
Desire for advanced precision,
And a bit of Refined FIRE mixed with Refined ICE.

Please, my Honourable GOD, make us all the best that we can be
Here on Earth, Eternal Human Family
Forever in LOVE ...

STAY NEARBY, PLEASE WATCH ME GOD

My dear GOD,
I could tell You all about all,
But I'd rather watch with You
The screen of life.

I need a glass of Tea Divine
If You don't mind ...
I need to swallow my compassion and my passion
For human life ...

Watching the truth, I'll cry! I know ...
I cannot cope with all the pain, visible on our globe ...

I know it is necessary to upgrade the global race,
To turn its face towards the light
From the deepest cosmic night ...

I am with You, my GOD!

I love, I sacrifice, I plan,
I prepare for every trip,
I shape the dreams that should go deep
In my simple human mind.

I will work smart!

I will take charge of every chart,
I'll straighten the oblique,
I'll impress, I'll intrigue,
I'll caress, I'll press
The page of every file of desire ...

I'll print my mind for other times
Before You call me home ...

I'll be OK my dear King,
I know what changes I shall bring ...

Please send me angels for protection,
Smart answers to every question,
In regards to global love ...

Stay nearby,
Please!
Watch me GOD.

THE UGLY TRUTH

Never in my life will I mention
A devil or his expression,
Nor, will I ever take any tension
From a corrupt!
A fake!

It is my life!
It is my mind!
It is my love!
That I will share as I will please
Only with smart,
And kind.

I'll never be the blind!

I'll never be attacked!
By the one that lied
In order to attract.

Gossip away Devil of Dark!
Just take your barrels off your mind
Before your truth and lies collide.

Smelling like good aftershave
Pretending to be all that's brave
You rotten, vicious Shark of Dark!
Today, from my clean mind, I will erase the hurt!
Your evil mark.

You drunken bastard!
Faithful to The Darkest Gods.

Never ashamed to go ahead,
Calling yourself "family head!"
When your child swallowed knots
And big tears, instead of bread.

Now I'm mad!

You don't need muscles of steel,
In order to hurt, to kill.

Just a stupid ugly brain!
That breathes the air in vain!
And the lowest intellect
Of a monster imperfect.

MY DEAR CHILD

You are the angel of my mind,
From you ...
I learned how to be kind ...

My sweet angel, morning light,
I hope I taught you what is right
In life's game of Peek-a-Boo
That is absorbing even you ...

When you will sip life's divine wine,
Remember darling,
You are NOT mine ...
You belong to GOD!

Through cosmic times, my dear child,
You are Forever Loved:
By your dear ones ...
Your babies ...
Friends ...
Pets ...
Many humans ...
Family ...
Angels ...
Me ...
GOD ...

By LOVE itself.

TODAY'S ADVANCED MEN

You Gold Collar Angels of Love,
You did succeed!
And did confuse
The traffic of divine in me!
And surely I'm after you
In my romantic poetry;
As I should be!

CHILDREN'S BEST NEST

Many children have been hurt
By insecurity fields,
By the family concept,
The war of minds for the perfect
In every aspect.

Long time ago, in my small past
I watched my family's own blast
Spreading the troubles everywhere
While curled somewhere in there
I cried the tears of every child:
It isn't fair!
It isn't fair ...
My dear GOD!
This world is wild!

Mommy!
Daddy!
Where are you?
I need my blanky ...
I need you ...
To tuck me in,
To tell me stories ...
Cry to me your major worries ...
Just please don't leave ...
'Cause I'll help.

Look at me!
I'm a big girl!
I'm a big boy!
I'll never ask for another toy!

I'll be the angel that I should ...
I would daddy!
I would mommy!
I would!

These small angels need to rest
On daddy's lap ...
At mommy's breast ...

Young and old,
We all need peace!
We need respect and love, the cream
Superior in every dream,
To complement the cosmic sky
Every time we say hello
Every time we say goodbye
Or, welcome back to paradise!
My human spouse, full of advice.
Let's try again!
It could turn nice.

Reunions can work, be sweet ...
Dear parents,
You'll succeed!

Children can grow up embraced
By human love ...
The love that is so highly chased
By an entire human race.

The dilemma being:
We all think, we know the best
Comparing to the world, the rest.

My dear friends, mothers and fathers,
I know, you'll do your best.

Start again and think it slow
Before you take the chance to blow
The safest nest.

Calm today is in great demand
In the family's stressed land.

What can we do?
How can we play?
The game of life,
The game of love,
The parent's game that is so tied
To success or to disaster ...

Today who fails looks like the monster
Of the inferno.

Oh dear GOD!
Help us absorb
Whatever will be good for us!

Please!
Empty our every glass
Of lust and vain;
It only brings disaster!
Pain ...

We will create the wonderlands
For these young spirits, fragile minds,

We will play comedies together,
We will make promises that matter,
We will be clever!

Please help us GOD.

IN THE WORLD OF RELIGIONS

Oh Mama, please!
Oh please, let me sleep and rest,
I'm too sick to do my best
I suffer from way too much pain
From being hurt, from being chained
Over three decades in vain,
By someone who has no shame;
What's his name?

I know it's Christmas,
It's church time ...
Go ahead!
I'm doing fine
In my bed.

No Mama, please!
I cannot come
To listen to the great elan
Of all those men you know so well.

Mama! Listen! It's my bell!
My call to GOD, my dream of peace
That for so long I really missed.

I'll stay in bed. I will get well.
Will you understand me, please?

I love you, Mama!
You know that.
I know your drama,
We did chat
About life's game taking the blame
For every hard inflicted pain.

What was that?

I should listen to you?
Baptism only will take me to heavens in your view?
Your church is the best from all of the rest?
The Bible is holy and true?

Of course, dear Mama ...
Whatever you say
Will happen to sinners
Who refuse to obey.

The church does minister
The pain and the blister
Of ignorance, the evil sinister?

Pleasure's highway is large?
But it is not the main—Exit from pain?

Who's final selection will be problematic?

Oh Mama ...
Let me tell you!

In the world of religions
Nothing is true,
Nothing is fake,
All is perfect
In a dream imperfect.

Say Mama!
Who is correct?
Who has the right to infect?

Mama, Mama ...
The future of minds needs hopes ... vision ... kinds ...
Not narrower blinds!

Our GOD is just one, The Powerful Force
Who gave us the love, the truth, the remorse!
Who is visiting minds day in and day out
In search for the smarts in conditions of drought.

Our GOD is The Father of all global humans,
And proud of ITs crop, the vast intellect
Continuously reaching for future perfect.

Mama! Our GOD does take care of us all.

GOD kindly fills glass after glass,
Of every human rich or poor
With cosmic wealth and love ...

Even the pain that I've endured, GOD will erase ...

I love the fact that GOD is The King of The Universe
The Father of The Global Race.

Believe me, dear Mama,
In the mind of our planet
There is a global church!
Where every human cries to GOD!
Where every human feels adored ...

Oh, dear Mama ...

GOD implored
Our human race before
To STOP the metaphor!
And write the facts more clear ...

But humans ...
Engaged in delir ...
Stubbornly continue to ignore
The GOD.

GOD LOVES THE PEOPLE

GOD loves the people!

GOD created us all.

GOD loves the flowers!
The future is ours!

A petal for you,
A petal for me,
A petal for GOD,
One for history ...

THE EARTH IS QUIET AT NIGHT ...

Only the trains and the planes are still shaking the Earth
And the skies ...
Heavily loaded with supplies needed for humans ...

A wolf starts howling,
The Moon laughs at him!
Without any rest
A bird in her nest
Is having a dream
About a worm crawling
Up on her chest.

I look at the sky and I pray to our Lord
To give us smart dreams,
Dreams we aford,
Dreams of success ...

We need answers about the mysterious rivers of DNA ...

I'll love to dream more ... I pray ... and I pray ...

Tomorrow I'll continue my plans.
Good night, my Global Friends ...

Look! The sky is offering a kiss!
How sweet ...

From behind a tiny cloud, the Moon is spying like a fox,
The stars caught in the paradox
Stuck to its lips ...
Cleverly, they didn't miss, one kiss.

CANADA
THE ROYAL BRIDE OF SNOW

Beautiful Bride of the North
My love ...

The roses in your hair are white,
The colour of your eyes, blue bright,
The magic in your voice is calm ...
I love your charm!

Kings and angels want your hand!
Strangers admire your land!

You, The Royal Bride of Snow
Let me tell and let me show!
To the world ...
Your magic bow,
Of snow.

Your arms, long and slim
My Lady Divine,
My Lady Sublime ...

My CANADA,
Designed by GOD to dance with Lords of many worlds,
Between the words of global fire swords.

A GREAT LEADER IS GREAT ART DESIGNED BY GOD

When the future of our country is at stake,
Let's make no mistake!

Fight with every fiber there
For the good that we all share,
For the essence we inherit
Give the heroes their merit!

Kiss the ignorance goodbye,
Don't ask why.

Please everyone!
We cannot rest!
We need leaders!
And the best!

Remember the brave? The smart?
A Great Leader is Great ART!
Designed by GOD.

Let's work towards perfection
In every single election.

Don't sleep on it,
Maybe ...
I might ...

Stand up and vote!
VOTE right!

YOU, CHARMING GLOBAL MEN ...

My love for you is running wild
I laugh alone like a small child
I walk asleep in snowy nights
The stars and Moon my only lights,
The snowflakes melting on my face
My mind has left the Planet Grace!
I'm wildly in the mood to chase
Your love,
Great Global Men ...

The wind is acting like a fan
It trips me over the Snowman
With the ever freezing plan,
To STOP me from loving you,
It turned me into ICE!

Oh, boy!
My love for you, is a heavy price.

By morning time no longer froze
The Sun will give me another rose
Of light,
Or gold ...

My life will be a brand new show
Of love ...

The global love we know ...

Good night, honourable Global Men ...
You are Forever Loved ...

GLAMOUR ... AMOUR ...

BEAUTY and LOVE, Flavour ...

All carried by cosmic times
Through the fires,
Through ice,
Towards the human shore ...

It's late ...
I washed myself with Baby Dove
I brushed my teeth with minty Colgate
I feel so fresh and so in love,
So ready to enter the gate
Of night ...

The Q10 Nivea I used
Did penetrate deep in my skin.
I hope I'll dream to be amused,
I hope that my high adrenaline
Will make a deal I can't refuse ...

It did ... and said:
Tonight ... your dream ... please keep it clean!
Don't look for love's excuse!
Obey the night!
Wait for the light!
Refuse the alluring voice, without any remorse.
You have to learn the need to grasp,
And the delight of pause ...

Good night, my Global Friends ...
Dream clean, healthy, beautiful and fresh ...

THE KEY TO LOVE'S OWN GATE

Good night, my loving Global Friends,

Tonight ...
Please dream of being loved ...

It snowed in CANADA, so I think,
For me ... love will arrive quite late ...
There is more drama on my plate
With every nordic blink.

Why would I cry?
What for to die?
When cosmically it's understood
My passport towards the fair
My contract with the life's own flair
Spread on every cosmic plate
That holds the fruit.

My access to the only key,
To LOVE's own gate ...

I FORGIVE YOU SIR

But now ...
I'd better think about a kiss ...

About a hug ... that I will miss again tonight ...

I'm lonely.
So lonely that I want to cry ...

Someone else somewhere on this planet
Feels just like me tonight,
I know ...

Or ... maybe,
Maybe I just remember that someone said so.

Ah ha!
I remember who implanted the thought in my mind!
It was my divorce lawyer, Mr. J.W.

I forgive you, Sir.

THE NEW YEAR'S EVE

My Global Friends, the New Year's Eve is close,
It will come with celebration, with Tam! Tam!

I will be alone again ... without my king ...
Maybe champagne ...
No love ...

No one to kiss my lips ... Me ... The Lonely Poetess
Dreaming ...

My mind for global love is screaming!
For laughs, for cosmic/human life,
More light for those asleep
So deep ...

It is my fault, I know! I know!
I never call on telephone
I do not tell that I'm alone,
I left the world!
I live secluded under the gold poetic sword
Designed for me by GOD, The Lord.

It is so late ... By 4:00 A.M. I'll be in bed,
I'll dream of being missed ... of someone kissing me on the lips ...
Dancing around The King of Kings
It would be fun ... I am convinced ...

I'll fall asleep in my dream's own arms,
My present king of love and charms.
Happy New Year! My Global Friends,
Love, love ...

TONIGHT I CRY

Love needs to be seeded,
Love needs to mature,
Love needs to endure the rules of life.

In my case,
I'd be OK with a fine dream tonight ...

But in dreams love is not real!
It can't be shared!

I'm scared ...

I walked outside a while ago,
The Moon was up and prominent,
The sky was solid and potent,
The stars in charge with the large cosmic field ...

Down on Earth we humans build
More rules ...
That we live by ...

Tonight,
I cry ...

I DREAM OF BEING KISSED

Right now,
I dream of being kissed ...

I know!
I know!

No one is here ...

I will imagine one!

A hero of the Northern Sky
A soldier who believes in love
An angel of The Great North Pole
A Canadian man in love with life ...

THE HEAVENS ARE WATCHING US

Let's get organized,
Let's be selective,
Stay healthy and loved,
Because my dear friends,
We're being bugged!

The heavens are watching us!

Oh, please!
Let's spare GOD from all the human antic fuss.

HOLY STRUGGLE IN THE JUNGLE

I'll hug you like a lion in the poems,
OK?

Tomorrow I'll be the lamb, I'll let you breathe ...
The day after I'll hug you with more love,
The day after I'll caress you with more calm,
And so on ...

Let's love passionately:
Like lambs ... Like lions!

You! All of you who are a bit aggressive,
Please! In love, you have to be progressive!
A lovey-dovey attitude
Is needed, in order to elude ...
Otherwise the heavens cry with human tears of:
Why, why, why?

The magic could freeze!
The globals could miss
The lamb and its calm ...
Or your glamorous feline charm ...

I know it isn't fair!
But when tempted, my dear Sir, Madam,
Use finesse ... use beauty ... use calm ...
Unless,
You're locked in the great garden with a lion sick with love.

I can sense the holy struggle
Being played in every jungle of divine.

WE LOVE THE FROZEN FIRE

We Canadians are filled with the fire of love and desire.
It must be something that this North is doing to us.

Forget the skis and Grizzly Bears,
We are the Polar Lions!

We are the Lambs of Snow ...

We love to rule the Ice and Fire!
We love to love the Frozen Fire!

We are The Global Models,
We're filled with Nordic Love ...

Good night, my Global Friends ...
Goodbye ...

Go dream ...
Of your own Ice and Fire ...
Of global desire ...

Of love ...

I LOVE THE WAY YOU HOLD ME

Your arms so relaxed ...
Wrapped around my sensuality ...

Your mind so strong ...
So in love ...

I feel safe ...

Your intelligence smells like power, Sir ...
I don't think I've ever been more intrigued by a man ...

That's why I smile ... just as you do ...
At love ... At power ... At intelligence ...

Reality makes me believe
That in this small hallucination
Are two humans, YOU ... and I ...

We are a complete unity of the infinite truth
At least for a while ... on Earth ...

Regardless,
I'll always love the way you hold me
Tonight ...

For the rest of my life I'll preserve you in my dreams, my dear Sir,
And I know that you will dream of me ... beyond power ...

Through cosmic times
We will remember our brief interaction
In the world of attraction on Earth ...

WOMEN FROM AROUND THE GLOBE

I see the efforts you invest
In building nature's sweetest nest.
Your smarts are bringing out the best
In every human chick.

Your breast feeds the world,
You bend and you fold,
You scream in great pain,
You brake every chain,
You listen to cries,
You pay every price
In heavens ... and in inferno ...

For being family protector—You lost the elector!

Don't take it seriously, friend ...
Please re-group!
Go do your best! Ignore the silly stone-age spell,
You are cosmically adult!
You know it well.

Hey friends! Psst! Come here please!
Let me show you what you missed:
Perfume, seduction,
Fatal attraction,
Fashions, some light,
Walking at night,
A hat ... or a feather ...

Do you really think that some of this nonsense matters?
Naah ... Not that much.

But, let's have fun now anyway, OK?
Take a glass of champagne,
Let's cheer and let's dance!

In your mind ... Twist the arms of the dark!
Stop if you can, its evil bark.
In the dream ...
The jungle is ours, covered in flowers!

GOD is just ONE! The It All Sublime ...
Do you see any extreme?
What extreme?

While out there, look out for the night!
In your heart, enjoy the brave, the bright,
'Cause it could be your daughter, son.

Madam ... You helped produce the global clan!
Now, please enjoy the cosmic fun.

My dear Global Lady,
Customize your life: Travel. Enjoy your family and society.
Be fashionable. Work smart. Build wealth. Read. Have fun.
And, think of what I said,
"You are a cosmic adult—You're travelling on your own cloud."

Good night ...
Go dream ... Love men ... Read my poetry and laugh ...
Prepare for the Refined FIRE ...
Remember that you are Forever Loved ... By GOD ...
By unsuspected humans ...

My Honourable Global Ladies, I wish you love, success and luck.

LIFE'S LONG TRAIN ...

I'll wear the hats of Peek-a-Boo in every dream,
I will parade for you!

I'll bring the planet's kindest people to calm you down,
To kiss your lips ...

Do not forget!
Postpone your trips, until tomorrow night ...

In Canada it's late ...
It's night again ...

The cold is chasing me in vain,
By love I'm being slowly warmed,
By winter I'm being alarmed
That I'll be cold on life's long train ...

My love for our human race
Is digging deep for its own place
In this human heart of mine ...

My darling cosmic/human friends,
Your love is tall ... divine sublime,
The illusion ... is ... your dream ...

Good night again ...

Stay warm ...
Remember life's cold, long train?

Go love!

WEDDING IN THE UNIVERSE FOR VALENTINE

It's night again ...

Tomorrow,
The Sun will shine forever bright
To warm us all until the night it will scream,
Let's dance!
It's Valentine!

That's when the Sun will fall in love
And steal the Lady Night a kiss
Wrapped in divine ...

There will be a wedding in the universe
For Valentine.

My Global Friends
Let's dance!

PLANET EARTH
THE SHINING GALACTIC STAR

Born for a divine destiny,
Beautiful like poetry,
Filled with charm and mystery,
Shining Galactic Star
Seen from afar.

Legendary Jewel
The greatest human school
Of universal love ...

Earth,
Our home ...

How much we love you,
How much we need you,
How much we appreciate being your children ...

Beautiful, beautiful Planet Earth ...
In your arms we dream,
In your arms we play,
In your arms we love,
In your arms we pray,
To never ever die.

Out of love for you
Our special Mother Earth,
Tonight ...
We, your global children
Cry ...

SILENCE ...

Deep, deep silence ...

It's dark outside ...
It's night ...

No souls ...
No Moon ...

I'll be asleep quite soon ...

I'll dream the light out of the dark,
I'll press for morning hopes,
For melodies that would attract
The cosmic/human jokes
Of love ...

Good night ... Go love ...

Yes! You!
Not me!

I'll only dream of human love ...
Of one small kiss ...
On lips ...

AFTER I DIE

After I die
I'll visit my Global Friends
One more time ...

To serve them Champagne of Divine
To whisper love in their ears,
To caress their faces,
To give them a kiss ...

To leave a cosmic tear on their pillow
As a symbol of how much I will miss
Being one of the ordinary humans
On an extraordinary planet
Designed with so much love in mind ...
By GOD.

I BELIEVE I'M BEING LOVED

The Earthly sky is jammed with stars
My radio plays my favourite theme, Star Wars ...
My heart is heavy with regret
Seeing myself, the lonely poet,
Without some human love ...
Who cares?
If I'm alone ... So what ...?

I'll go to bed in a few minutes
Forget my jacket and my boots!
Forget the starry sky!
Why cry?

Tomorrow is another day!
I'll be good! I will obey the law of GOD ...

I'm sure that I will receive
Some secret love and I believe
I'm being loved ...

But now ... Now, alone under the sky
I'll say I love you and goodbye
My cosmic/human friends ...

Under the feathers of this night
I'll dream of love claiming its right
Of residing in my heart ...
Maybe a kiss ...
From someone I do not know,
So, I don't have to cry ...
Or miss ...

I DREAM OF SLEEPING BESIDE YOU ALL LIFE

I dream ...
I dream of being in your arms
I dream of your enormous charms
I dream of you ...

I dream ...

I dream that heavens will be fair
I dream of receiving my share
Of love on Earth ...

I dream ...

I dream that smartly you and me
Forever play the Peek-a-Boo
In the world of déjà-vu ...

I dream ...

I dream of a better cosmic clue,
Supremacy and grip on love,
Fire burning the barricades
And set the human mind all free,
You and I forever mates
In the garden of illusion,
Super-love, final conclusion.

I dream ...

I dream of sleeping beside you ... All life ...

THESE DAYS I SUFFER ... I DREAM ...

Your mind is here beside me ...

For now and for eternity
The two of us we'll be in love ...

At night I close my eyes alone,
Unaware I do condone
Your instant presence in my mind ...
Then stubbornly I do reject
Being kissed, and I protect!
My right to be alone ...

But your mind from love's own throne
Grabs my arm!
Surrounds my waist!
Then with finesse gives me the taste
Of being loved ...

All my life I have been chased! No reason to invent.
And I did manage to protect
My honour ...
And easily preserved,
Respect.

But your love, my dear Sir
In its innocent attempt
Succeeded to twist my mind ...

No longer stubborn,
No longer strong,
These days I suffer ... I dream ... Like any other human.

THE REVELATION IN MY DREAM

I'm on my knees ...

I pray to GOD for love ...
Love for the entire human race ...

Then I ask,
How in the world will I do my best?
At night ... why do I need to rest?

A few minutes before midnight I did fall asleep ...
The night had carried me so deep
From Earth,
To the universal mind ...

I felt the love of our GOD
Caressing me so kind ...

The midnight had just passed. I started to dream ...
A new day with its agenda started to unfold
Yet, I continue to dream ...

I dream between the reasons of divine ...
With my invisible mind
I try to scroll for love ...

Suddenly I'm part of a huge gathering!
A large convention centre. A reception.
Many famous politicians, guests, media, police,
All interacting ...
From the crowd, a tall young officer gently took my hand
and kindly asked me to walk with him.

He guided me outside the building where The Sun was waiting ...

There, I was given a silvery hose and asked to splash crystal clean water in front of The Sun.
I took the totally weightless huge hose and I started playing ...
The colours of the rainbow started to show through the water ...
The Sun started delivering a sensitive, powerful glowing light,
A light I'd never seen before in my entire life!

Even though divinely shocked and surprised, I asked the officer,
"Why do I have to play here?"

"Because it is your job to have fun.
The Sun wants to be entertained by you."

"The Sun wants to be entertained? By me?"
Secretly, I laughed ...
"Sir, but can The Sun see that I'm not a child?"

"Yes! The Sun is a living entity. A very smart cosmic entity."

Wow!
My job is to entertain The Sun?
To play with It? For It?
With crystal clean water?

Then, I thought again in secrecy,
"Really, isn't my age an issue here?"
My mind would laugh again,
"I'm not that young."
It sounds a bit curious, yet who am I to question the reasons?
Especially those of a very powerful cosmic entity,
Like, The Sun.

I will comply! I will play! After all, I am an artist.
Even if it sounds unbelievable,
I believe that my play is meaningful.
Cosmically meaningful.

See?

This time could be my season,
My love could be the reason,
My poems are the water,
The rainbow the smart ladder
The message crystal clear;
In fact, the cosmic thrill
Is the game of light!

The splendor of It All being that
For me here in this life
My only option to deliver love,
Is through the game of fun!

Playing outside the crowds,
Alone ...
Just me and The Great Sun.

Now I really feel like a child in wonderland.

I know that no one minds me playing in my global corner.
It is an honourable corner!

My job, just like my mind, is beautiful.

For the rest of my days,
I'll dance and I'll play,

I'll pulverize crystals of love
For The Sun every day,
And for you ...
My special Global Friends ...

For you and for those involved in important global meetings.

DEAR ARTIST

I feel your pain, your mind's ardour,
I see your talents in your art,
I sense the torture in your heart,
And yes, just like I said before,
I'll pose for you a little more ...

Prepare the fur, the fireplace,
Some champagne ... and take your chance!
Painting illusions in advance
Could help you dream!

You never know what the Sublime prepared for you!
Maybe a dance under the Moon
Maybe a kiss in a cocoon
Filled with divine ...

Don't laugh, my friend.
Just paint!

And yes, I really love your voice ...
What a tenor!

You sang for me in the restaurant,

You treated me really elegant ...

I'll always think of you with honour, my dear Sir.

How much amour do you think I really need?

My dear Sir, life is placid!
I do adore you even more seeing you artist timid.
I love you, Sir.

HON. JOHANN SCHMIDT, MY MENTOR

Fictively,
A young girl in love with the powerful mind of a great man.

This afternoon your great embrace
Drove my mind to other times ...
Far away ...
Where I could prodigiously chase
Your mind's empire, cosmic grace.

It seems like yesterday, my Sir,
Yet, is so deep in time ...

I loved those times, my dear Sir.
I loved your mind.

DEAR MR. SECRETARY

You young delicious angel,
You hold me in your arms today ...

You measured my waist
Then quickly you placed
Your hand on my breast ...

I wish I was free ...
Alone in the nest.

If the heavens will reserve for you
Another dream in magic-land
Then, you could play
And could pretend
To hold the magic ball ...
The secrets of It All ...

You make me laugh ...
Young angel,
Sir ...

DEAR TYCOON

In your strong arms, I get the fever!
Love's own virus at its best
Takes control and makes me shiver
Under Earth's magical sky ...
Tell me why?

One thing!
May I suggest that ...
How should I put this?
Please write a little protocol
That you'll be able to obey,
And keep your lips under control,
Regardless of the play.

No French kissing!
Not today.

My Sir, you did intrigue me with your incredible French dinners ...
Your business success ... Your multilingual skills ...
Your heroism ... Great politics ... Patriotism ...
Mega million dollar deals ...
Satellites and sub-terra projects ... Fibre optics and networking.

Your world?
A world of great romantics!
Your dreams?
The infinite of heavens!
And its splendor.

I sincerely love powerful men like you, Sir ...
They help humanity.

DEAR LAWYER, DR. FUN

I don't even have to blink when I tell you what I think
That you hide!
A mind filled with passion,
A heart of compassion
A kiss that is mine,
A moment of ours
That should be divine ...

I love the snowy, sunny days on Hwy 401 ...
Because of you!

By now, I've learned to watch the ... EXIT
No longer can I afford to permit
My mind to wonder so far away
Minutes from the border to the USA.

If it was for you,
That day, we could have ended up in Chicago, Sir.
And coming back,
Pass Toronto and end up in Montreal,
Exactly as you said!

My love for you is special, Sir.
Thank you for the fun memories ...
For the Scottish royal stories ...

For describing so divinely
A British soldier's love and mind ...

You silenced my spirit for a moment that day, Sir ...
I'll always love you for that.

DEAR PUBLISHERS

My friends of ages ...
Publishers of every thought ...

When you hold my hand through times,
I proclaim ... t'was elegant.

DAN

You went to GOD ...
Young ...
But not before transferring great skills to your sons, your friends ...
To me ... a stranger who freshly arrived from a refugee camp,
pregnant, with very little English, without money, without a family.
The world of publishing is what you loved. And love itself ...
Classical music, dance, your family, and Dor, your beautiful lady ...
After a distance of a few years, one day I had a premonition.
"Call Dan. Call Dan."
I called to speak to you, when D'Arcy, your son, told me that you
were not home.
Then, I asked D'Arcy, "Where is he?"
"My father died yesterday."
What a shock! I was guided towards the celebration of your life
at the funeral home in downtown Brampton.
Was raining outside. Elizabeth and I find you in your final bed:
Your beauty devastated by colon cancer.
Your body covered in white flowers.
We cried ... You left too soon.
You are in heavens now ...
Thank you, Dan, for the inspiration, trust, guidance and friendship.
You are Forever Loved.

LYRIQUE LYRIC

Couverture of confusion
Son of music
Flamme of illusion
Amortisseur of control
Diamant of the conscience
Magique of the mind ...

AMOUR ...
LOVE ...

Allez! Allez!
Go away! Go away!

Adieu ...
Goodbye ...

Revennez! Revennez!
Come back! Come back!

Fleur d'esprit ...
Flower of mind ...

MARIANNE - THE TRANSYLVANIAN PRINCESS
vs.
BOB - THE ANGLO-IRISH PRINCE

He—The Anglo-Irish
She—The Transylvanian
Embraced in fiction's finest war?

I heard this argument before!

GOD the King did this for fun,
No reason for paravane!
No more.

The truth is exposed!
The case will be closed
In regards to
Who loves who.

Let's clarify why!

Every Irish man I see
Is very attracted to me.

Could it be?
That mystic of ages
From Stoker's lost pages
Are being upgraded
Wherever they faded
Preserving the fire
Of Bob's great desire
Of meeting with me?

Reality vs. Fiction in Elysse's Mind—CANADIAN Poetry

I tell you ...
I do know him very well!
From other times,
From other trains,
I know also the other names
He mystified, when a female
Kissed him on the neck's love veins
Leaving him in great suspense,
For a while ... not too well.

Near Bistritz, I can swear!
In Petersdorf, where I grew up,
Where he wasn't too aware
Why the village was hung up
In love's net, where no map
Showed the place.

Let me tell you why that truth is immense,
'Cause,
I was there!

Watching down over valleys perfect clean
When a train well camouflaged
Carrying a man in green
Started going in reverse ...

That was him!

Bob was there looking for me!
My love ...
My hand ...
My poetry ...

This Anglo-Irish, love's tycoon,
Looked there for me a little soon!

His heart was on fire
His mind wrapped in wire
Of love and desire.

This fictionist crazy for dreams,
He travels the universe
Sometimes even in reverse!
Confronting the magic rhythms,
I'm convinced.

In this chase,
He climbed the Carpathians for the place
Where he dreamed that there might be
Transylvania's Princess,
Mystic me.

Every Green Spirit then was told,
Watch for Marianne, please!
She's the mystic truth unfold
And the love I always missed.

That's why to this day,
Verify!
You may!
With every step I dare to take
Another Irish friend I make.

They have emotions around me ...

What could it be?

For almost eight thousand years
Bob never stopped searching for me,
In desperation to receive
The kiss that I don't want to give
To just one man,
But the entire human race!
And I believe deep in my heart
That Irish men are very smart,
But also, look how they can chase all sorts of love!
Almost ... like me.

Bob's fever forever will burn!
Irish, Transylvanians,
Fiction's best comedians
Embraced in love's custom inferno.

I AM Marianne!
I'll teach you the game of love's greatest fame,
Just pass me the kiss I want and I miss ...
Do you hear me, Global Men?

Not on my neck. You silly!
Don't force me to keep you in check.

As for the Irish men, I care
That history wasn't quite fair ...
Instead of running love's own school,
Fiction remains their best tool.

Look my Global Friends! How Bob, the Irish Prince of Love,
Is landing in the world of passion,
Proclaiming his kiss the fashion!
To attract me to his net—I can bet!

You Devil of Love don't be mean!
You're not even in red!
You're all dressed in green!
In a clover of luck hangs your dream.

You cosmic romantic in need of "that kiss,"
Keep trying! I bet you will miss!

And so, the fiction continues ...
Bob, the charming Anglo-Irish Prince of Love, forever chasing
the young and beautiful Transylvanian Princess, Marianne.

ELECTION

With every event
I gain the percent
I need to inspire.

Fundraising
Dinners
Celebrations
Power
Money lubrications
Roads too slippery to travel
Sickness cured with VOTES and Gravol.

Not a big deal!
Just an ELECTION!

Embossed in luck,
Into perfection.

Miracle! Without a question.

IN LOVE WITH THE POLITICIAN

I will pretend
To be your friend
Clean and correct
In a world "so perfect ..."

The love I feel for you
Is driving me insane!

What can I ever do
To stop dreaming in vain
Of one more
... déjà-vu ...

Encapsulated in your magic
I will love through ...
Hypnotism!

I know exactly it would be tragic
Never touching realism
Through the dream of optimism
Called humanely, romanticism ...

Romanticism and idealism
Are viewed through the cruel custom prism,
Are open book to criticism,
Cyclone of Hearts
Without pardon!
Politicism.

The price is immense
The ardour intense

The atmosphere tense.
No love for us ever. No chance!

That's it!
It is clear!
No reason to cry in past tense.

But let's just imagine no prohibition,
Nor the sharks of opposition
With the ever dark ambition
To ruin ...

Regardless,
I'll hold that feeling
So supreme ...

Your eyes filled with fire
Of love and desire
Forever will spark in my dream.

I'll burn flames with fire
Chain love, with its wire
Stop the dream with your fame
In the name of the game.

All politicians in the world,
Smell the flowers of your powers
In the garden of your fame.

Stay safely loved, Sir ... Madam ...
Smart Global Leaders ...
I bow to you ... as I EXIT
Your secret pain of restrictions ...

YOUNG SIR ...

Young Sir, you are so irresistible ...
You display so much love ...
I look at you and I do dream of seeing you loved.

I dream as all the poets do:
It's all a game of Peek-a-Boo
Of love's own fire
Forced to wire
Humans, two by two.

Watch your back, smart lover boy!
The hooks are floating in your waters,
Soon, it could be you!

Find someone to kiss today,
If not? The back of your own hand is good for practice.
Go ahead! Start to imagine the girl of gold,
There ... in your bed ...

Don't swear at life!

If you play right or play some more,
It would be impossible that your heavy resources of ardour
Would not attract the right contract
Of love on Earth ... Designed specifically for you ...

Call it marriage ... Peek-a-Boo ...
Have a pick!
Just remember! Play! Play! Play!
Stay in love with every day!
With all that humans do obey in this great life.

WHAT A LIFE

Filled with pain
And filled with struggle,
Like a coffee double-double.
Sugar, cream, the heart attack,
Here and there a little luck,
A tinsy-binsy shred of love ...

But you know what?
With the release of the Refined FIRE
Our love and hopes will rise.

Wait a minute, you smart guys!
The girls are also in the game!

Once equal,
No one can blame
The human nature
For inventing the torture.

Let's dissolve the insult!
So, NO ONE has fault.

OK?

CLEAN YOUR MIND AND CLEAN THE PLANET
IF YOU COMPLY, EVIL WILL DIE

The sweet innocent memories of the times when pure cosmic love
overwhelmed our minds as children, forever will live within us.
That is the seed of light and love!

Dear Global Friends,
Withdraw the purity of light and love you used to feel,
The innocence of simple dreams when you were all ...
Not this or that,
Because someone, along your age, said that you are,
Or you should be ...

You are just fine! You're made of love!
You're flowing in the poesy
Of light's time ...

No cosmic mind has ever had a skirt!
Or pants!
Or feathers to impress!

The cosmic mind is all progress!
And love!

The cosmic mind is clean!
Is pure!
Refined in every aspect!
Capable to shake the Earth
In order to connect,
In order to address
The semi-cosmic human mind
Stuck in antic mess

Of long passed lazy human times
Or stone-age crimes.

Oh, poor, poor times ...

The food humanity needs first
Is EDUCATION!

It is the biggest thirst!

The global children love perfection!

In fact, recently I had a chat
With The Honourable GOD
And I was told:
Extend your hand!
Do not just pretend
To do what is right
In your deliverance of love and light
To the incubator of my fragile young minds on Earth.

Decorate their rooms! Tell them beautiful stories!
Feed them! Protect them! Stay vigilant!
Keep out the evil!

If you comply
Evil will die!
Evil is old!
The FUTURE is shiny and bold!

Evil doesn't matter.
In its blindness
It can parade any feather.

Me, The GOD, I do not condone
Any more primitivism,
Dictators or communism,
Hate on Earth without pardon,
Or silly, naive criticism.

And here I could be prone
To impose some realism:

Clean your mind
And clean the planet!
Clean your house
And clean your habit!

Keep control of your smart moments
If you want to avoid the torments
That could come.

Listen, dear human package!
Use your calculated calm
A bit of your cosmic charm
From your cosmic given luggage,
Your infinite mind.

Do your best to interact!
Use smart strings, please,
Go extract love from the earthly human mind
If you expect me to be kind
In my act.

Listen carefully my children!
LOVE is choice
EVIL is noise

LIFE is action
DEATH the attraction
Of another cosmic time ...

What is it?
You call yourselves smart girls? Smart boys?
Ha! Ha! Ha!
Did you ever hear ME voice such division?

Do you think I operate on choice?

Hmm ...
Oh, please!
Go back to that smart mind that I give you!

Choose to memorize the phrases:
Humans need to be more kind,
Humans mustn't be so blind
To the smartest cosmic future.

Anyway ...
Because some of you did well,
I'll lock the evil in its cell!

I tell you all that I Love You
I'll share with you the Refined FIRE
And for as long as you will live
Remember that,
You are FOREVER LOVED.

MERCEDES

I dreamed last night
A Mercedes
A Mercedes
A Mercedes
It drove me through life's repertoire
Towards the shore of love ...

My love ...
Shall we drive to the Stratford Festival today
To see great Canadian acting?

I'M BLIND WITH LOVE

I'm blind with love ...

Being as blind as I can be,
I ended searching the Black Sea,
Down at the bottom of its sand
I lost my hope to understand,
I lost control and I'm not through
I'm viciously in love with you ...
I cannot see.

Now, with sea weed over my eye,
I'm sure, I will pass you by!
I cannot see.

My mind is really scandalous!
My twisted spirit, furious!

Up on the mountain of despair
I find hope's own magic chair,
I sit on it and I declare:
Love is something we should share!
To help shake off the marine wool,
To help us see ...

I'm blind, as blind as I can be,
You're strange, as strange as destiny,
You're not aware of my great pain,
My mind is courting you in vain,
I'm blind with love,
I cannot see.

THE NEXT BANQUET ON EARTH

The next Global Banquet will be
A thrill for all of you!
For me ...

We will enjoy via Light-Waves
The screen of magic set in place
To charm us all.

Above the head of every country
The mirrored truth will play us back.

We'll learn much faster. We'll learn plenty.
We'll learn exactly who we are!
Through shock.

The lessons prepared are much needed
To wipe the tears, to end the horror,
To implement the needed honour
Humanity so much desire ...

Trust, progress,
Great Refine FIRE
Of love will be delivered
To all!

That day the global protocol
Of how we shall obey
Will be engraved in cosmic gold!
Then, openly it will be played
Provoking humans to be bold
And to agree!
To love It All.

THIS GOLD COLLAR ANGEL OF LOVE

Today I reach a final decision!
After torture comes ambition.

I'll never ask for love again!
I'll never suffer so much pain!

I was refused a little kiss by a glamorous adult,
What an insult!

GOD knows, I'm not at all amused
Considering how he infused
His magic fire right in me!

Then, started to disagree,
Leaving me on love's own floor
Discriminated and abused,
Without the kiss that I could use
To help me dream ...

This cruel crime
Beats any time
In history of human kind!
Its equations magnitude
Of passions that so smart elude,
Seducing humans with illusions
Promising love's own soft cushions in small print,
But not the kiss
That the humans, so much miss ...

This Gold Collar Angel of Love
He did succeed! And did confuse!
The traffic of divine in me,
And surely I'm mad at him,
As I should be!

Sir!
I've never been so hurt in life!
And let me tell you here flat,
You played with my love's apparat.
I'll never ask for another kiss!
And I won't chat!

You'll have to court the roots of love right out of me!
To force me measure one more rhythm,
To admire your hormonic lips
Filled with sacred politics—You stubborn Serafim!

And yes! I'm not finished yet with you!
Forever the accused
Who shamelessly refused
To kiss me when I want.

Oh, Lord! Please help me to resist this Angel Elegant.

I'm secretly in love with him!
That's why I cry
Not knowing why
I find him so sublime.

He's torturing me day and night!
Is this normal? Is this right?

I should confront him more and say:
You Love Dictator! You will pay!
For crimes you did commit.
I'll wait for you, just one more night!
If you don't come, I'll say goodbye
Until another life comes by,
In which ... you will be mine!

I swear to GOD!
That it is what
I'm hiding in my dream.

Forever zapped by love ...
In this life we daydream poetically ...
Of that illegal kiss ...

In reality we shy away ...
We miss ...

We ask ... we can get refused ...
And ... we feel like little criminals ...

I suggest that we relax ... kiss, kiss ...
Laugh at ourselves ...
Before we miss completely the magic of life.

WE ARE SPACE TRAVELLERS HAVING FUN

We are in the garden of our Sun, in its playground ...
The Sun is caressing our global soul with its golden beams of light.
In secret, it is warming our minds.

We travel the universe with such elan ...
We are space travellers having fun.

Look at the speed that we travel with!
The cosmic wind refreshing our cosmic memories ...
The beautiful planet Earth dancing around the Sun,
Maintaining the rhythm ...

Who are we?
Do we know? Do we need to know?
Would we like to know? Should we know?
Is it necessary to know details?
Are we ready to know the details?

My beautiful Global Friends,
We are the infinite—We are the day and the night,
We are the dreams of the future,
We are the love—We are the drama,
We are blending with the universe.

We are FOREVER LOVED by One Fine GOD.

Let's stay loved in every sense. Let's be good! Let's love life.

Let's be kind and honourable towards everything.
Let's be an example in our space.

This life is our private seat
On this fine vessel that we did embark
To generate love and peace ...
To dream
Fine dreams ...

Let's build a reputation by saying that
Our space ship is the most honourable in the universe
To travel on.
Let's show hospitality to Lady LOVE,
And Lady LOVE will bring more LOVE energy on board.
It will bring cosmic tourism to our planet.

LOVE attracts LOVE!
Let's fall in LOVE with LOVE
Today ...
And forever ...

Please!
Let's never STOP the cosmic dream!

We need quality energies not only to visit us on Earth,
But to find residence here on our planet.

We need the Refined FIRE,
The LOVE of LOVE.

LONDON ...
ENGLAND ...

You City of London ...
You England, the country ...

You and You,
The historical light
Of minds global loyal
London ...
England ...
The royal ...

I compliment you here
Not because I must,
But because it's true!

Your mind is brilliant!
A mind I trust.

You honourable royal parent of the global power.
The greatest conciliator—The super communicator
On Earth.

I did discover that you are
My linguistic inspiration,
My poetry without a question.

From CANADA
Today I'll say,
Thank you.

It is my honour ...

I HAVE A QUEEN, QUEEN ELIZABETH THE II, QUEEN OF CANADA

A royal child, the child of King George VI and Queen Elizabeth,
Sister of an attractive cosmic princess, Princess Margaret ...

Glamorous bride of an elegant, generous prince, Prince Philip,
whose honourable desire to protect her is forever unshakable ...

Mother of four beautiful children who quickly arrived from the
four cardinal points, equipped with prestige ... ready to intrigue ...
Recipient of precious, wonderful grandchildren ...
The joy of her life, the charming youthful royal future ...

I have a Queen!
A Queen who loves the planet,
The Queen of Commonwealth, with friends all over the world!
A Queen who loves people,
Heroes, wild flowers, smart dogs, brave horses ...
A Queen who believes in GOD!
A Queen who prays for peace and tranquility
For the entire human race ...
A Queen who is admired, and loved ...
A Queen who rules in honour.

I am Canadian and I have a Queen!

A brilliant cosmic spirit, a noble I trust.
An extraordinary global model,
A model of royal honour and love ...
Love for beauty ... Love for peace ...
Love for life ... Love for all people ...

THE HONOURABLE PREMIERS OF ONTARIO
SPRING 2002
AT THE MISSISSAUGA CONVENTION CENTRE

Hon. Bill Davis was,
Hon. Mike Harris is,
Hon. Earnie Eves will be ...

One is attracting—One is departing—One interacting ...

What an honourable show!

Dear Sir,
Tonight ... you are the magic of the hearts,
In history ... you'll be Forever Loved.
I wish you well, I wish you all the best,
And ... I'm intrigued by that ... poetic side of yours ...
I love your spirit, Sir ...

My dear Global Friends,
Please love the smart leaders that we have in the world today.
I myself love my good leaders.
Look! I even write them love poems! In secrecy, of course ...
And why not?

Pssst! Please don't tell! They have no idea!
I'm not quite sure if all politicians read poetry.

I knew a Bobby Kennedy who did!
A Pierre Trudeau who showed us his flower of love's power;
Furthermore, he amazed many with that swinging coat of his.
But these famous leaders, the U.S. Democrat and the
Canadian Liberal, have left the honourable global building.

So, the actors I choose to be, love's best slaves in this poetry,
Are the rulers of today! They are alive!
They are the leaders that I know.
They function hidden in armor
Of refined secrets.
They have charisma and control!

And ... boy! They have that magic warmth.
They carry the fire
I chase, I admire,
I dream, I desire
To touch, to extract
To explore, to attract
For my poems only, of course.
Can you see that all our global leaders need sincere love?
It helps them in their: expressions ... emotions ... devotions ...
They have to court us all,
For our VOTE!

Please, let's maintain the theatrics
To enable them to produce the charm.

We need them!
We want to keep them healthy and happy!

Of course that they see our dance of pretend,
But at least they relax, having us all condensed in one friend,
"The PARTY."

To my extraordinary leaders, one ... by one ...
Honourable, Sir, Madam,
You are Forever Loved,
By many globals ... By me, the poetess ... By GOD ...

I LOVE YOU, SIR

Dear Sir,
My love for you did grow with time, I love you so ...
I love the spring of your perceptions,
I need your magic, your attentions,
I need your love ...

I'm eating strawberries tonight ...
I'll dream of landing in your arms
Without putting that silly fight
Pretending to ignore your charms ...

I came to terms that it's all right
To tell you that I love you, Sir!

It's getting late ... I'm off to bed ...
My love for you will be all spread
Over the magic of this spring ...

Oh, Sir ... The bells of love finesse will ring
Deep in my mind ...
Until the Sun will call for wedding
Forcing me to stop pretending
That is fine without you here in my bed ...
And some fine Niagara wine ...

Listen, Sir ...
A funny bird delivers songs at love's request:
Oh, my love ... you are the reason,
Oh, this time ... it is the season,
For reviving human love.
I love you, Sir ...

I DO BELIEVE THAT
I DO HOLD ... THE PEN OF GOLD

I hope to print my mind quite soon ...
If ... I'll remain shielded in this lagoon
Covered by the waves of life ...

From time to time
I'll dare to dive
For thoughts that swim in every dream
That I receive
Between mysterious range hertz
Indicative of reverie
Access to the memory
And the smart lucidity
Of time ...

My dear friends,
I do believe!
That I do hold
The pen of gold.

I'm in the world,
Yet not of it.
Intrigued a bit by it's paranoia,
Oh friends, my dears ...
Now, I'll dispense of life's euphoria ...

Aaah ... I feel delta's ultra slow momentum
Clearing my mind ...
I tricked myself once more ...
I'm fine ...
I am asleep ...

WHO NEEDS A POETESS? LIGHT'S PRINCESS WHO DREAMS REFINED PROGRESS

Who needs a poetess in his life?
To write him verses day and night,
To treat him really elegant ...

Could it be?
Someone who accepts existence in the light
And the divine commandment
Of love?

Someone who can accept
A cosmos innocent
Engaged in the survival fight
With humans who don't understand
The infinite with its concrete Divine ...
Mathematically aligned ...

Someone,
Who's looking for finesse ...

Who needs a poetess
That acts like a princess of light?

Hmmm ...

Let's see!
Someone just out of his own sorrow
Who appreciates human existence,
Someone who trusts in a tomorrow,
Someone who understands persistence
And the divine cosmic chase for Refined LOVE ...

Could it be?
A champion in human kinds, a cosmic mind that smartly blends
With human minds?

A king, who's not afraid to rule
The domain, the cosmic school
Of Refined PROGRESS?

A king who will deliver
Elites to be considered
The cosmic/human experts in new refine design
Of cosmic/human kind, The Refined MIND?

Could it be?
Could it be an artist? The hidden invisible
Who appears convincible
In how he strokes the human mind
With all those brushes, so divine?

Or ... A wine expert in the field
Of numbing human minds!
Just for a while,
Until The Great Divine
With the greatest cosmic smile
Could play ITs magic
Reducing the tragic
To a ZERO pile.

My Honourable GOD,
Who needs the poetess that dreams Refined PROGRESS?

Please tell me, my dear GOD, believing in human smarts and kinds,
Is it just a lonely dream of mine?

IT'S VALENTINE AT THE NORTH POLE

Alone ... without a single soul ... no love ...

I cried today thinking of passion,
I ran outside, I flipped on ice,
And now, I have a small concussion!

I guess that LOVE does have a price.

It's RISK that we assume to take,
To get the LOVE, the Earth we shake!
And then, of course, there is no question
That the candy of temptation
Is equally being shared:
One bite for you, one bite for me,
Peek-a-Boo ...
Sweet destiny ...

I can't allure wrapped in this fur!
I want a fashionable dress!
Let's spray some perfume and prepare to impress.

Then, we will embrace—we can go dance ...
We can hold hands ... We can be friends ...
FOREVER in LOVE ...

It is February 14. It's VALENTINE at the North Pole!
A bit of drama here and there, just enough that we would care,
And learn to appreciate the good ...

My dear Global Friends, Salute!
From your Canadian Polar Friend.

I WISH I HAD A HAND TO HOLD

Alone, it's true,
But free and glad
To have peace here in my bed ...

Tonight,
I dream as humans do,
I wish I had a hand to hold
A lover along which to mold
One more night ...

But the reason of one's dream
Is to have a little gleam
In the idea of total comfort
Which some humans cannot afford.

So,
In my case, I'll stay alone.

I'll just dream ...

I'LL WAIT FOR YOU

I'll read the oldest almanac
I'll listen to Johann S. Bach
Until you'll bring me the white rose,
Take my hand and hold me close,
Give me the kiss I so desire
And set my cosmic mind on fire!

I'll wait, my Sir ...

ONLY LOVE WILL VINDICATE THE HURT

Dear friend and dear neighbour,
Have you ever been in labour?

Going into labour is like going to war!
Both ways we risk our lives.
That's the cost we pay the most,
Both, MEN and WOMEN.

That's how our Solar System was created!
Through LOVE and SACRIFICE!
Through BIRTH and WAR!
The ultimate price.

Right now the world just hurts a little.
Trust me! We globals are the human native,
Sincerely, we are quite creative.
Together we are all strong!
And intelligent as long
We remember that One GOD
Is the only King we've got.

Regardless of the hurt, we all stand up today,
We look together at the sky
And pray ... And pray ...
And pray ...

We cry ...

My Global Friends, let's be alert!
That only unity in progress, peace and global love,
Will vindicate the hurt.

Intelligence and competence
Are needed!
To help the world progress,
To give us the access
To the divine basin
To a future clean
Filled with everlasting love ...
And peace ...

The peace that we all miss and need,
And cosmic beauty!
That is so splendid
To touch ...

LADY JOYCE

If I had the vastest choice
In choosing friends
Here on this globe,
I'd start again
With Lady Joyce.

She's made of love!

Her soprano voice
Indeed,
Is the friendly note I need.

LADY MAXINE OF LIVERPOOL

So classy ...
So elegant ...
So fashionable ...

With so much expertise in Victorian style ...

Maxine,
My beautiful blonde friend
With her unique smile ...

Wise words that commend
Blending of global fire ...

Lady Maxine of Liverpool,
One of the finest Global Friends.

OKAY, DADDY GOD

GOD is on the line with all the babies of the world.

GOD: Hello! Hello! Hello my babies! How are you?
How is your earthly playground?

THE BABIES: Daddy! Daddy!
Here we all play the game of Peek-a-Boo
Between the fields of Beta, Alpha, Theta, Delta ...Gi! Gi! Gi!
While the adults keep an eye on everything we do.

(In fact the parents have no clue, what the babies think or do).

GOD: Oh, my tiny darling babies,
Make sure that you pass the clue
To those adults playing so tense
In this fine game of Peek-a-Boo.
Teach them:
Cosmic fragility, responsibility, sensibility,
Meditation
Contemplation
Resistance to tension.
Teach them that love is the strict order!
Teach them not to cross the border of temptation.

All of them should learn the passion in life's labour,
After all, it is the flavour shared by every cosmic neighbour.

THE BABIES: Okay, daddy GOD. Ba-bye!

Cosmic click.
Secretly, the children are in charge with the cosmic reception.

I'LL BE RIGHT THERE, MY SIR

Talking to myself ...
If I stand the ground and just turn around
Ignoring the passion, the classic concussion of time ...
This silly moment maybe ... it will pass ...
I can't do it! I have to talk to him!

***

Hello my Sir ...
I call 'cause I'm a bit confused!
Since you began to hold my hand
I began to understand
That I want you near
And I love you dear
All over my mind ...

Do you still want to serve me a cup of Earl Grey tea?
Yes?
... OK ...
Will we watch the stars tonight?
And drive around the city?

What else?
... I see ...
I like surprises! I'll be right there, my Sir.

I'll bring the wildberry pie,
Some memorized good verses
Written specifically for you ...

I can't wait to see you, Sir,
I will be there.

YOU ARE A HERO, SIR

Alone ... with the historic memories of life ...

A candle flickers beside you,
A flower stands half dry,
Your wife has died recently
And you are asking why?
The time is cruel ...
Again ...

Half asleep ... holding a book of war,
There is no trace of lust in you.

Sir, please let a fresh day start
In your lonely life.

In your tired mind, let go of the past!

I know, Sir, I know ...
That's why with my mind I caress your face ...

I know your acts of good intent,
Your book ... the best historic trace
Written by your tired hand ...

Survivor of the darkest blast
You escaped the past,
Yet another time
You remained
Alive.

In verses of hope I can hear your voice ...

Honourable Sir,
Because you were designed to employ
Courage, and destroy past heavy ignorance,
You did miss a portion of this life's romance ...

During World War II,
All that you enjoyed
Was bringing the progress
To global access.

Even today, my honourable Sir,
A candle,
A flower,
A book,
Is all you possess ...

And a heroic, romantic great mind of gold ...

I thank you Sir,
For the beautiful world ...

You are Forever Loved
By all those who understand ...
And of course by me ...
And The Eternal GOD.

A FRIEND, A ROSE

The truth of fairness she carries
The mind of GOD she simply married
The fashions of her rusty clothes
Make extra special my friend Rose.

YOU CAN CHANGE THE WORLD

We, the talented humans:
Scientists, writers, musicians, journalists, actors, comedians, sports people, teachers, doctors, law professionals, architects, smart commentators, technologists, environmentalists, strong military leaders, smart business minds, trade professionals, business minds, farming specialists, modern spiritual leaders, balanced politicians.
Mothers, fathers, children, brothers, sisters, grandparents,
Then ... the extraordinary neighbours ... good global friends ...
We, together, are the truth on Earth.
We, my friends,
We know that the individual can change the world of perception.
The individual makes it better!
Always was and will forever be about the individual.

History, cultures, religions, gender, colour or age,
Should not paralyze our future as humanity!

We are invisible spirits, yet we choose to materialize in this human form and we adopt rituals which often are culturally based, and not entirely complementary for the good of IT All.
Remember! If we can stand up alone, and I suggest we should, then, we can stand up in any cosmic society, any existence!
A individual's strength can have more positive effect globally than an entire procrastinative society! (Historically proven lesson).

It is about the human created in the image of GOD,
The black and white and all other tones between—GOD.
The negative and positive poles—The IT All, the ultimate light.

The one respecting GOD is in the business of love!
And LOVE is GOD residing in humans, the universe of It All,
In you ... In me ... In eternity ... Forever!

THE STARS TASTE THE NIAGARA WINE

Tonight above the Canadian land
The cosmic colours largely blend,
The sky is dancing so divine
The stars taste the Niagara wine
Agreeing that love should be fine
Tonight ... on our globe.

The Canadian vibration, the perfect connection,
The bit of its heart, attracting the smart,
Its honourable mind, linking the kind
Around the globe ...

The things that we say, the price that we pay,
The tears that we shed, the thoughts that we spread,
Provoking debates,
Are all a reflection of how we obey ... of how we love the globe.

And here we do risk!
Tonight, in dream we do implore
The globals we so much adore:
Please! One more kiss, one more embrace,
All your love, the love we chase ...

Together, great stars of love, we could all breed,
Great moments, we could well conceive,
The future, is what we believe,
Great honour, is what we'll receive
For raising together the global flag of peace.

My special Global Friends,
So long!

IF WE'RE REFUSING TO EMBRACE THE MIND OF GOD

There is no chance for misery to last!
Therefore, my dear Global Friends,
Let's crack the stiff cast
That keeps us paralyzed in the total nonsense of the past.

Let's start! Get organized!
The future is approaching fast!

Today, let's be together smart,
And avoid the final blast.
It could take place!
If we're refusing to embrace
The Mind of GOD.

Please! Don't look back!
We humans need to look ahead
If we want heaven's smartest bread.

Apocalyptic poverty, does not bring humility,
But death!

Let's swing from A to Z today,
Make sure that we all obey
The law of GOD.

The Constitution of It All
Will never fade!
Will never fall!
The human race will have success
If dreams in terms of great progress.

THE ROLL OF GODs ELITES IN THE DESTINY OF OUR WORLD

Welcome to GODs Plan!
All global issues are in the mind of The Supreme.
ITs elites on Earth, calmly ruling, mostly in secrecy ...
Some players, occasionally posing for the covers of smart magazines ...

The debates taking place day and night
Behind the curtains of thought ...

Few, selected global policies publicly displayed ... To feed the need ...

Overall,
The order in the universe is being followed
At divine speed ...

Today,
The position is tackled
The insignia buckled
The flags are displayed
Rules are obeyed
The order is settled.

All the advanced
Are taking the chance
To sit down and ask
For the next global task,
The order that matters.

Some globals agreeing,
Others scared fleeing
The order.

GODs elites are in charge
With matters at large
For better, for worst,
They filled every post
Of order.

It is GOD that decides
Without taking sides.

It is GOD expecting the best
In every great test
From the smart globals who understand the great need
For order.

GOD chose ITs elites for now here on Earth.
Since we know that the process of global rebirth will be complete,
Why not dream?
Why not follow the order?

Today, around the large square table,
I heard from from the leaders of the world,
It's order.

Through history, once in a while, successfully,
Fresh new elites are elected,
The global power erected
By GOD,
In order.

Now, the honourable leaders of the world
All under GODs microscope,
Are being pushed to the extremes by heavy decisions
And new policies of the cosmic order.

Their minds well designed to defend
And to proceed with the global order.

It is GOD who gives them the shoulder
In implementing and preserving
The order.

It is GOD who will upgrade the global mind overall
To help humanity follow
The cosmic order.

The honourable humans of today
Prefer progress and order!

They go with the flow,
Down the river of the cosmic order.

My dear Global Friends,
Look closely at the globe ...
You'll find GODs decision embossed in children's minds!

They dream ...
Global progress ...
And order ...

OM, YOU MAN ON EARTH

Om, om, om ...
Man, man, man ...

What are you doing omule?
Why are you dancing all alone?
Shouldn't you hold a hand?
Display a bit of strong back bone?

You omule!
You man!
Oh, let me help you with a plan:
Just like the global infrastructure,
The blueprint of the bluest planet,
The trail of great love's departure,
The tail of the fallen comet ...
You have a hand!
And a mind to understand
That all you have to do is stretch!
When you sense a perfect match.

Om ...
Man ...
Go out there and hold a hand!

EDUCATION

The greatest temptation on Earth,
Education!

Law,
Mathematics,
Chemistry,
Physics and astronomy,
Zoology,
Anatomy,
The advanced biology,
Social studies and religion,
Histories of every region,
Geography, geology,
Fine art and photography,
Cinema and world's best fashions,
The fabric of global passions,
Theatre and literature,
Ultra new architecture,
Global arts of every sort,
Olympics of every sport,
Science and technology,
Transcendence ...
My poetry ...

Oh, my Finest Global Friends ...
How good it feels today to be
The best that we can be.

This mind bugging protocol
Is the mother of
"It All."

Dear Global Friends,
Grab the information
'Cause good education
Helps in transformation!

We'll be fine if we agree
That this very poetry
Is the zapp induced with calm
Intended to guide, to charm
Those capable of smart dreams
Who'll dance according to the rhythms
Of a perfect universe
Embedded in every verse,
Subtly provoking the temptation
Towards a higher education.

You glorious humans ...

Go learn!

YOUNG SIR, MADEMOISELLE, CALCULATE THE ENERGIES!

Parking lots above the cities
Highways towards the heavens
Slides that penetrate the oceans
Speed without the time of limits,
Jackets used to lift the humans
Trapped on Earth that is on fire,
Energy without a wire!
Resides in us!
And can be measured!

Up to now, it was well treasured ...
(*Thank GOD*).

Cosmic Biology=Gravity
Cosmic Energy=Mobility
Cosmic Chemistry=Activity
Cosmic Mind=Eternity
Eternity=Transcendence
That was, that is, that is to follow
FOREVER!

Please use simplicity!
For gravity, use perfume, good food, commodities ...
For mobility, use an energetic car! A bicycle! A boat! A jet!
For activity, use chemistry. Get a job! Get married! Have children!
For cosmic-human contact, use magnetism and transcendent thought.

Desire things with all your mind and your wishes will materialize sooner or later. Pray to GOD with honesty and humility. Oh, please start! You can change the world in a better one.

IS THIS LIFE YOUR MASTERPIECE?

My suggestion?

Do your best
And plan perfection
In your future of intention.

Cosmic nest
Without a question
Is the ground.

Any galaxy out there
You can choose ...

But please,
Prepare!

Any world that can be found
Could publish your new life's story.

Be aware!
It needs some magic!
Otherwise its extra tragic
Could give others too much worry.

Do your best!
You won't be sorry.

It is within your hands,
My friends ...

HONOURABLE GLOBAL SPY
SIR ... MADAM ...

Clubs based on psychic adventure,
Minds based on architecture
Of cosmic power ...

Remote viewing?
Private lecture?
Goal?
To scan the globe for those
Who naively could devour
The peace on Earth, the perfect rose
Of a future now in flower?

This power takes sacrifice!

Abstinence from interaction,
Psychic muscle in contraction
Preserved intact for the great cause
In its future of intention,
Beyond the sphere or the dimension
In the transcendence of It All.

Minds of powers inconcrete
Trained until they become elite,
Capable to keep the finger above those that could delete
Future progress.

And some would!
Many innocents of nature, if no one is trained to STOP them,
They naively would devour the progress!
The dilemma being—How can they know, if they don't know?

My Global Friends,
Trust the smart spies!

These humans dressed to mesmerize
Are at risk, for you and I.
They pay a price!

While travelling the globe
They might look like modern mob
Mixed with powerful and poor,
Never tired of the tour
Of discretion.

But these shadows of impression,
From the bottom of the ocean
To the highest planes we know,
Keep an eye on the commotion
On the road with life's great show.

Even I with great devotion
Keep the game alive and well
By preventing the extortion
Of the fortune parallel to the notion:
That Les Canons de Pachelbel
Awakens the 7th sense
A world of wonder so immense
That could indirectly scare
The innocent, who could not bare!
The emotion.

My Global Friends, be smart! Prepare!
Never STOP being aware in this game of Peek-a-Boo
That is involving all of you.

Go and read!
And read!
And read!
Knowledge is the most splendid
Treasure, in the cosmic luggage.

You'll learn a thing or two of why
Heaven pretends to apply
The infinite commandment
To our stable sky ...

In the mean time, my Global Friends,
Let's respect and let's admire
The Honourable Global Spy.

Read their stories!
It could be your son ...
Your daughter ...
Your father or mother,
Your friend ...

Or ... even your lover!

You'll never know.

Sir, Madam,
Honourable Global Spy ...

WE'LL EXIT FINALLY THE PRISON OF CONCRETE

Our dear GOD,
You give us knowledge ...
You give us vision ...

From sky to sea,
We know, we see.
From heart to heart we feel the beat,
From eye to eye we see the clip,
The cosmic network of the mind
Projecting hope in humankind.

How in the world we wrote the books?

While in dance with the perplex
We managed to simplify
This giant pile of complex.

Oh, GOD, we're shocked we qualified!

With patience, we simplified
The puzzle flying all around
Faster than light, faster than sound,
Accessed and understood by few,
While the rest left without a clue
Of its existence.

But You taught us, dear GOD
That with persistence,
With trust in all that we admire,
With proper use of ICE and FIRE,
We can go higher!

'Cause we love the concept of this scope
We'll fight!
We'll pass the envelope!
This telepathic policy
To the great humanity.

Even today,
We cannot resist but ask ourselfs
Between the twenty-four and twelve:
Why every bit appears in place?
How the division of time's space
Gives day and night the equal chance
To travel mind's own universe
Ahead,
Around,
And in reverse?

To live
To love
And to devour
Futures calculated hour?
To slap the past with its own future
To slash its time with its own butcher
To swing the mind from A to Z
To speak without an interpret ...

And in conclusion:
To reason finally the reason,
To exit finally the prison
Of concrete.

Dear King of The UNIVERSE, please ...
Help us sort, understand, and accept the complexity of It All.

AT THE GALACTIC TABLE

Acceptance of progress
Clearly will enable
Our human race
To find its own place
At the GALACTIC Table.

This honourable spot
Is just a tiny dot
In the book of GODs intention
In releasing our tension
Giving us the Refined FIRE
Wrapping us in love's own wire
Carrying us between the stars
Far away from earthly wars ...

My dear Global Friends ...
Keep dreaming!

EVIDENCE OF EVOLUTION

The COSMOS now has evidence
Of our human competence,
And therefore, in the divine courts
Humans are needed as consorts,
As guides in areas of thought,
The one thing COSMOS will adopt
As a Cosmic Policy
Inspired by humanity.

Thought of love
Thought of compassion
Thought of beauty
Thought of fashion
Thought of romance under the moon
Thought of great love in the cocoon
Of night ...

Thought from every human verse
Will travel the universe
For the angels to enjoy
For King Cosmos to employ
Human nature.

Oh, my dear Global Friends,
Buckle up for the adventure
In this joy.

WHAT'S UP PUNK?
I'LL TELL YA CHUMP!

Garry: Yo punk! What a' ya sayin'? What'z up?

Larry: Yo chump! Let's chill tonight!

Garry: Where?

Larry: Here in Brampton at Matrix, on Kennedy South, ... or Jack Asstor's on Queen Street East, for a celebration of the French Quarter's world famous festival, Mardi GRAS Festival, like in New Orleans.

Garry: Cool man! See ya at Jack's.

Larry: Yo Chump! Tomorrow, we go to Mandarin.
Then, in Orion Plaza
There at the CINEPLEX to chill some more.

I got paid today.
OK?

Garry: Sure punk! Cool, cool. Can't wait ...

SIR, YOU ARE BEING ADMIRED REMOTELY ...

Welcome into my mind, Sir.
Welcome into my telepathic dreams ...

At night ...
I'll share with you the illusions of my mind ...

In secrecy ...
I'll gently caress your forehead, Sir ...

Ah!
I can see you!

You are wearing flannel
My honourable Sir ...

Outside is snowing ...
You just put on some love music ...

You're holding a glass of rare French wine,
Watching the fire ...

Alone, yet satisfied with life,
You're smiling ...

I think ... I'll spend some time with you tonight ...
You cannot see me anyway!
I am remote, yet around you,
My Sir ...

Oh ... you are so beautiful, my Lord ...
You smell so good ...

You are a Lord I can't afford!
Soldier of forces of desire!

My Sir,
You set my mind on fire!

Enormously provoked
I suffer now from shock!

Oh, Sir ...
Listen to my remote whisper ...

In dreams land as a foreigner
You're being loved from every corner
By Princess LOVE ...

By me?
Remotely only, Sir.

So, please relax.

I am the poetess and I suggest that you stay beautiful, my Sir.
Dress elegant at night,
And remember!
You're being watched.

Always open the gates of your mind ... for Princess Love ...
Whoever she might be,
Globally ...

My honourable Sir,
Never forget that you are being watched
By Queen Femininity ... Remotely.

AT 17
I TOOK AN AMAZING RISK

Amazing risks I took since when
I left the nest of youth,
Reaching the point of adult
Life became quite smooth,
And secret.

I learn to listen and to care,
I learned to do my best,
I learned to laugh and love regardless,
In my new adult nest,
Of secret.

Youth of our planet!
It's fun being an adult.
Don't be afraid!

Just be yourselves and do your best.

Please try with trust
Regardless of the secret.

YOU, THE DIVINE AND EVIL

You, the one capable of creating beauty,
You, the brute!

You, the one forever secretly on duty,
Today, have my salute!

I'm out of here!

Your flame is dying.

I stopped thinking of you
And I began my flying
Away from those dark nights
Filled with tears,
With false compliance,
In the infinite effort of trying.

Your constant, constant jiggle
Between Divine and Evil
Does not translate success!

I believe that your unique, slow progress,
Made you Divine and Evil.

You really lost your spirit!
You no longer impress.

That's why!
Today,
I'm out of here!

What's shocking to me is:
The pride evil can trigger
The drive of a deceiver
The absence of regret ...

What can I say, you stranger?
This poem, "your portrait,"
Displays the balance you desire,
The sharp extreme of ICE and FIRE,
Divine and Evil.

See?
I do understand!

How about you?
Can you see that now, forever
You lost your closest friend?

PLANET EARTH, THE GALACTIC BEAUTY

Here at home on Earth
Life is so delicious
Lots of kids and parents
All are so ambitious.

Peek-a-Boo! I love you!
Cosmic tree,
My galaxy,
Planet Earth, the galactic beauty,
The galactic beauty,
It is.

The future is for children
Life is filled with joy
Cosmic friends and business
The planet does employ.

We have dreams!
We believe!
Aa, ah, ha!
Galactica,
Planet Earth, the galactic beauty,
The galactic beauty
It is.

Peek-a-Boo! I love you!
Cosmic tree,
My galaxy,
Planet Earth, the galactic beauty,
The galactic beauty,
It is.

MY LOVE FOR BRAMPTON

Forever and ever The Global City ... BRAMPTON

A city so new ...
A city of opportunity,
Love, beauty, prosperity.

BRAMPTON,
A city visited by the Honourable Queen,
A city were many books in modern history are being signed,
A city where science-fiction is being written,
A city where roses are part of the heritage,
A city serenaded by symphonies at night,
A city surrounded by lakes,
By rivers,
By forests on the hill,
By wonderful neighbors ...

A city where Shakespeare in the Park is being played!
Fashion shows, variety shows, and classic cars are everywhere!

A city where Bramptonians share their community love,
They share their laughs with all people. All globals.

In 1981 mainly European in descendance,
Bramptonians welcomed even me! The global poetess!

The theatres ... filled with artists interacting with the public ...
Receptions ... with wine ... elegant food ... and violins ...
Ladies in glamorous gowns ...
Gentlemen in black ties ...
Mysterious beautiful people ... searching for love ...

Reality vs. Fiction in Elysse's Mind—CANADIAN Poetry

Oh, my Global Friends ...
Pictures on the walls, global festivals,
Cute animal parks.

Brampton has its own Kinder Expert, Santa!
And then, of course, brave war veterans,
English Heritage houses, famous courts,
Health centers, hospitals, global expertise,
Variety of shopping malls.

World's most famous corporations continue to appear every day.
The space arms that famously massage the science news,
Come from Brampton!

Pearson International Airport is here at its gates.
Three level trains, modern transit, giant highways all around.
In Brampton, even horse riding is fashion!
The largest Ontario Saturday and Sunday Markets
Attract tourists with passion from everywhere!

In Brampton the art galleries, golf clubs, and restaurants bloom.
Here the fire fighters, the police force,
The doctors,
And the globally competitive culinary chefs,
Are in thousands! And number one in the world!
During holidays, dancing in the streets is natural!
In winter, skating at Gage Park is fashionable.
Even Hollywood loves making movies here in Brampton.

By 2010 Brampton was totally transformed, in a global city.
The minority groups become majority, my perfect global teachers.
Today, Brampton is a symbolic rainbow on the global sky.
This book is my written exam.

SESQUICENTENNIAL CELEBRATION
1853-2003

A historic celebration of
The Flower City of Canada
The Great Bill Davis' Great BRAMPTON
Poetic City of Love ...

The trail of beauty and the royal spirit
Stretched from Brampton, England
All the way to Ontario, Canada,
Where BRAMPTON was born
In the year 1853 ...

Today,
Brampton shines brightly on the blue Canadian sky.

THE CROWN vs. MY ENEMY

It's spring.
So many lawyers, coming, going,
My enemies, all so annoying ...

The weather is a big success
The great heat quite in progress
The sleek wind begins its blowing
Insects everywhere start showing
Canada displays its beauty
All around police on duty
Here at the court.

Overall my biggest question
Under this roof, full of suggestion
Is:
Why do those, I cannot mention,
Love the negative attention?

Dear GOD! What an invention!
You give us the beautiful lawyers,
All these fights, spouses, employers,
This courthouse, brilliant judges,
Charming employees wearing badges,
Liberties that are cut short
For those brought here in this court.

You made these part of the big game,
The honourable Peek-a-Boo.

I understand, Heavenly Sir,
I love it, too!

Her Majesty Queen Elizabeth II,
Defender of the Faith
vs. my enemy?

My Heavenly Judge,
What a great game!

For me,
This war of wars
It had to be!

I disagree with ANTI-me!

The poetess, illusive me,
Needs time to write!
Needs to be free
From naive dangers,
In order to create the needed divine poetry.

My Global Friends,
Are you with me?

MY ENORMOUS LOVE FOR PLANET EARTH

The planet ... is sincere!
Its virgin mind was designed to be loved by Lady ETERNITY
Forever!
Planet Earth is special!

Why?
Because it does understand how the globals blend.
Planet Earth is progress!
It is the basin open for access to the global mind.
Planet Earth is kind!

The Planet is adept!
Its mind can adjust. Its mind can accept the clear facts of life.
Our globe is a house of honour. This planet is alive!
A planet globals trust, and once they choose as home,
They revive ...

Planet Earth is LIFE at its best!
A fine, fine planet that is simply adored.
The map of its future is filled with splendour!
Super-cosmic beauty knocks daily at its door.

The Earth is the cosmic face,
This life is the dream we chase,
When it comes to family,
Just like this sweet poesy
Planet Earth is LOVE ...

This life attracts the bright at its side.
Satisfaction and honour is the attraction.
Security in every day and passion.

I LOVE NEW YORK

Famous city of integrity, City of Liberty
City of the smart and kind
The greatest blend of global mind,
New York ...

Massaged with every lotion
Of time ...

New York darling,
You have the energy to face your destiny.
You star of the world ...
You're fine.

From across the border
Have my poetic shoulder ...
As the poetess
I wish you success
And love ...

You city of fashion
Filled with love and passion,
Oh, you divine in beauty
New York, the tall
The greatest of all,
Your mind filled with emotion
Your heart filled with devotion,
You beautiful angel ... You're fine.

The heavens hold your hand
You'll stand forever tall
You are Forever Loved by the GOD of It All.

HONOURABLE GENERAL

If I may, Sir ...
I'd like to ask a question.
I'd like to ask, how often do you battle love?

Ah ... just a smile? The question, does not belong?

I know Sir ... that you are strong,
But please! Permit me to continue ...

Sir, your passion for global progress
Brought you up front in this process
And here, Sir, I do incline
To simplify the line.

May I, Sir?
... Thank you.

Across your mind my dear Sir,
I know the infinite you carry.
In war, love is your tricky cherry
That carries you towards access
To the passage that does take
Humanity out of its mess.

Honourable Sir,
The future ahead awaits for you
Dressed for the game of Peek-a-Boo
Wrapped in the heaven's softest flowers
Hidden between the midnight hours
In glasses of champagne and merry
Floating along with love's own cherry.

TORONTO, THE KING OF BEAUTY

Do you know that,
You fascinate,
You illuminate,
The global mind?

Your intensity
Inspires prosperity
Around the globe.

Your height
Brings to light
Your courage and strenght.

You, the greatest son of the greatest country,
Historically,
You did have your moments ...
Of pain.

And so, after all
Because of it all
You became more bold!
That's what I've been told
Last night in my dream
By GOD, The Supreme.

Fashionable Toronto ... Extravagant Toronto ...
You charming North American King of Beauty ...
You, the greatest Canadian metropolitan city,
You are loved by people from around the globe.
Your elegant romantic spirit is what we love.

THE FINEST GLOBAL FUTURE THAT WE COULD SHARE

Oh, my dear Global Friends ...
From a life so filled with pain
What do we learn?
What do we gain?

The planet is like a gold mine,
Where we suffer
Where we labour,
Then we have to wait in line
For some love, the only food!
By now, quite frankly understood
That we should share
With our neighbour.

But you know what?

Once united our minds,
In love and in the global kinds,
Could produce the finest future!
Envy of the Holy Sky!

Now, just between you and I,
Do we really need to cry
Any longer?

Let's dance ... Hold hands ...
Caress the fragile minds ...

We're GLOBAL, already my friends!
We are fine, honourable GLOBALS.

WE ALL ARE CHILDREN OF ONE GOD

The Moon is smiling through the pines
While I'm dreaming ... of the next lines ...

I write the poetry to you,
Sometimes I cry, I have no clue
Why I risk?
Why I love you ...?

I hope I entertained you well,
Now, go listen to Pachelbel!

Sweet dreams ...
Sweet life
My Global Friends ...

Please remember
To follow tomorrow's new cadence
Of truth ...
In everything you do ...

Please trust!
Have faith!

We all are children of One GOD,
Remember that!

THE DIVINE GOAL

My Global Friends,
The Holy Land is Planet Earth
The holiness is the rebirth
The baby is humanity
The divine goal is the integrity
That GOD in all of us
Desires.

Don't ever, ever, believe in division!
Stubbornness is limitation!
Nonsense argument!
Confusion!

GOD is running out of patience!

My dear Global Friends,
Be clever!

Snap out of the antic illusion!

FOREVER!

THERE ARE THINGS WE DO NOT KNOW

Cosmic love, continued flow ... is the only thing we know ...

Friends! Please wait for my revival ...
I need to recharge.
I'm running from a scandal,
A rumour at large.

Someone condemned me for visiting galactic lands!
Mirrored times, divided space,
Hidden states of mind's own grace,
Energies behind the dream,
Having fun sliding the beam
Up and down galactic glands.

Hmm ... Imagine that, my Global Friends!

Cosmic numbers, cosmic codes, all twisted in science knots,
Knots too hard to comprehend,
To sort them all, we do intend,
Don't we?

Oh, Oh, Oh ... So much complexity ...
That's why my friends,
We the globals should hold hands
While King UNIVERSE bends
According to the protocol
Over the fences of It All.

In this life we should go slow ...
Discover more ... Go with the flow ...
There are things, we do not know.

THE GLOBAL IN ME, LOVING THEE

The global in me
Is vowing this life
To Thee ...

My mind unique in all
Continues to scroll
In everything,
For Thee ...

My dreams are away
My heart wants to play
My mind jumps with joy
My thoughts are a convoy
Of love for It All,
Thee ...

The child in me
Is trusting
Thee ...

Thy is in charge
With It All at large.
My mind's nobility
Is kept secret from me
For now,
It rests with
Thee ...

All that I need to know is that, I'm global now!
I'm global! I'm good!
The plan is understood!
Thee ...

I MAKE LOVE TO AN ANGEL
I'M LOSING MY MIND ...

Since gifted with love,
I've been courted,
Kissed,
Embraced ...
My hand has been held,
I'm super-adored
By an Angel of Love,
A beautiful mind.

It all started with verses,
Love verses and music,
Music of love ...

Oh, clean, clear love ...
In your honourable cosmic moments,
Your powers are divine ...

Silence and motion,
Fire, proportion,
Blending emotion ...

Rhythm and energy
Perfume and poetry
Whisper and suggestion,
"The divine will be mine!
Tonight ..."

I'm floating in heavens,
In the hands of magic,
I make love to an angel
I'm losing my mind ...

The dream is projected
The rhythm is perfected
The fire is burning right across my body,
I drown in love's passion,
I cling to the moment
Enduring its torture, its wavering torment ...

Explosive desire!
Infinite fire!
So fine ...

A God and a Goddess
Make love ...
Embraced in love's perfection
Incapable to mention
The finesse that surpasses
The elegant mind ...

Energies embraced
In cosmic shock placed,
Agony! Dance!
Fire!
Infinite desire
To love ...

My darling, please give me a moment. Please, I need to depart ...
Sincerely, I need to reflect. I need to scroll my soul for trust.
I need to cry ... because ...
I've never been loved this way in my life ...

I never realized that this type of complete love can come to me.
That's why I feel like I'm losing my mind. I need to digest this.
In a moment I'll be back in your arms and fine. I promise.

The GOD of Desire sprinkles cosmic fire
Over my tortured mind ...
In struggle, the mind does not perspire,
It's just sick with divine.

The glory of this angel,
Its power, Its pulse,
Its energy, Its mind,
All mine to experience
Tonight ...

Feminine and gentle, I respond to his love ...

He's holding my body above the bed of dreams
With one arm ...

He's powerful!
I'm seductive ...
I'm all his!
And he's mine!
Tonight ...

Classical themes,
Synchronized rhythms,
Love and more love ...

More muscle!
More fire!
Inflated desire!
Dance and trepidation!
Arrows of the mind
Shooting flames of fire!
I make love to an angel, I'm losing my mind ...

Confusion, kisses, tremor,
The love that I miss,
Struggle for release,
Oh GOD! Save me please!
I feel again like ... like ... crying ...
Of love ...

This Angel of Love conquered my being!

Engulfed by Its fire,
I'm losing my mind ...

Oh, LOVE, LOVE ...
You secret cosmic entity, intelligent mind,
Because of you, tonight,
I'm loved and I love, like never before in my life.

Thank you, My Sweet Angel,
For the magic life ...
For choosing to be mine in LOVE ...

UNAWARE, WE KISS ALL NIGHT ...

Not alone, not anymore.
We dance to the notes assembled by The Gentleman of Music,
We listen to Richard Clayderman's Music of Love ...
All troubles of the world exit our minds ...
Embraced and quiet
We think of LOVE ...
We float ...

Privacy, peace, silence and love ...
We need ...
Comfort, Sun and nudity.
Not phones, TV, or silly company.
Not tonight!

Tonight we love again! We're smart.

We laugh at our uncontrollable smiles ...
Inexplicable emotions built up in piles ...
Progressive strings of fire continuously provoking desire ...
Repeated invasions of refined energies transferring love,
Paralyzing the body, controlling the mind, maximizing pleasure ...
It is important that we mention, without a drop of perspiration,
Denoting divine intervention, not at all human invention.

Why do we suffer shock?
Why do we fall asleep embraced?
Why unaware, do we kiss all night?

Oh LOVE ... Sweet, sweet LOVE ...
How powerful you are!
How forever you enslave our minds.

TO YOU MY LOVE ... AND ONLY YOU

You turned my life into a land of fantasy,
You turned me into a beauty, to match my poetry,
You rule over my love!

In a sign of honour,
I'll fire my poetic gun!
Thank you, my Sweet Charming Angel
For the greatest cosmic fun.

Without you King of Discipline,
My mind would suffer
From lack of smart routine.
Without your kiss ...
Love would be missed!

Your lips ... the roses in my dreams,
Your kiss ... the fire in Sun's rhythms,
Your arms around me ... love's smart wire,
When loved by you ... I want to freeze!
The FIRE.

It's night on Earth and once again,
Love wrapped us in its mystic chain,
I'll dream with you of global peace,
Romance in Frankfurt ... or Paris ...
Our LOVE ...
The pain we can't explain ...

I love the way you always hold me,
I love the way we play and laugh,
I love the way we kiss all night ...

My dear Global Friends,
Forget my tears,
Life is absurd!

See?
I discover that Frankfurt
Had long ago designed my love!

Today I think,
What do I know?
IT is GOD deciding all for me,
And I accept my destiny,
I'm privileged!
Look!
I can love!

From now on, my Flying Angel,
Let me tell you what I'll do:
I'll play with you, and only you!
The entire game of Peek-a-Boo,
In heavens and on Earth,
Forever.

POWERFUL MINDS

"It can be done!"
Is their permanent whisper.
"The planet will make it!"
Is their belief.

The ones who truly understand
Control the image of perfection
As their minds forever blend.

United, they create confusion!
Preserving the needed illusion
For the next cosmic debate.

Upgrading without intrusion?
Hmm ...

JORDY, LITTLE ANGEL

We miss you every moment
We love you every bit
We feel your spirit's content
We're honoured that we meet.

JORDY, tiny angel
You blue eyed, baby boy,
With your infectious smile
You charm us from a mile!
JORDY, angel boy.

You crawl across the planet
Chasing a balloon,
JORDY, little angel,
You will be walking soon.

You sit on Oma's lap
To eat your favourite food,
Then stretch your arms to Opa
Who throws you up, Hop! Ho-pa!
He makes you feel so good.

Your parents love you dearly
They show you to the world.
You forced them see life clearly,
You forced them to absorb
Love's essence and its good.

Thank you, little Jordan,
For coming to us all,
May GOD bless you eternally
Sweet baby, angel boy.

SENSIBILITY IS A QUALITY, UP TO A POINT

Sensibility is a quality, up to a point!
Sensibility prolonged and/or taken to extremes
can become a liability! A nightmare!
To any: person, nation, planet, galaxy, universe.

Complaints stretched over thousands of years can make us look ...
How?

Here, I don't have to mention other parts of the world, just the world
I come from and the world I belong to,
Europe and North America.

These two continents
carried the two greatest wars in the history of humanity.
Even seniors, women, children, horses, dogs and pigeons, fought!
... during ... and after ... millions died ...

Europe was flat on its face!
Every country involved was damaged, hurt, hungry, angry
and insulted to the limits.
By whom? By their own GOD given destinies,
destinies that in the end made them the greatest on Earth!
In war, good or bad, all people suffered! (Including the dictators).
Yet, these continents picked up the pieces and rose above the past
glorious, civilized, educated, fashionable, lovable
and kind enough to share their spiritual resources (strength)
and economic success (knowledge) with the rest of the world.
Now, that's what I call healthy attitude!

Perfection? Probably never.
Continuous love, kindness, prosperity and beauty? Always, forever.

AND SO THE COSMIC STORY TELLS THAT WE HUMANITY ... WE ARE ALL CHILDREN OF ONE GOD

I, Elysse, will forever love:
The global children and all citizens of this world!
The talented between us who do their best to help,
The magical minds that help humanity grow,
The business minds that invent resources,
The political minds that serve us by leading.

The secret elites that risk their lives daily for us,
The spiritually advanced reasonable guides, who console us,
The talented comedians that make us laugh,
The beautiful provocative artists that entertain us,
The designers that create our fashions.

The small rivers that teach us the rhythm of perfection,
The tiny kisses that make us smile,
The flowers that give us a sense of being embraced by heavens,
The trees, the oceans and the mountains that mesmerize us.

The sky that shower us with mystery,
The stars that help us dream,
The Moon that is nurturing our lives,
The Sun that is empowering our minds and reminds us of order.

The sweet/tough voice of the universe that is guiding us
telepathically through the mystique of the
Global LOVE and DRAMA.

I Elysse, will forever love the cosmic story that tells us that
We humanity, we are all the Children of One GOD.

OUR FUTURE

Our nest?
A corner charmed by peace.

Our work?
The policies we missed.

Our future?
Filled with mystery.

Our love?
The planet ... our galaxy ... existence ... music ... poetry ...
FOREVER.

LOVE IS

Love is the highest form of Cosmic Intelligence,
The most painful beauty of all existence,
The most mysterious truth of life
To LOVE we must.

BEFORE I LEAVE
I BOW ...
TO THE NOBLE HUMAN RACE

Before I leave, I bow to you ...

You, Cosmic Noble Human Race,
You honourably helped me dream
In human terms for The Sublime,
In exchange for infinite
Which will never be complete
Without the calling **I Love You ...**
The flow of cosmic **Refined Fire ...**
And the idea that we are **Forever Loved ...**

Elysse Poetis

CANADA

THE END

ABOUT THE AUTHOR

Elysse Poetis is Canadian since 1981 when Canada rescued her from a refugee camp near Vienna, Austria. She was born on August 8, 1953 in the *City of Literature*, Sibiu, Romania—the same year Queen Elizabeth II took her coronation oath. In 1980, at 26, Elysse escaped from behind the iron curtain to (then) West Germany. Today she is an Award Winning author/poet with numerous books available world wide.

I Love You is a 256 page book of Elysse's original poetry. It is Canada's universal fabric that made Elysse global. Her books are empowering, dramatic and humorous, recommended for all ages. She senses what will be of benefit to humanity and she writes with dynamism, encouraging and invigorating the human race. Elysse believes that her books are bridges of inspiration towards a better world. Excitement is what she wants to generate, and in so doing to plant the seeds of positive change, globally. Through her literary art the author transmits the idea of infinite cosmic life. Science is what she plays with in her poetry—and she preserves GOD as The Commander in Chief of all existence. Without fear of ridicule Elysse uses cosmic theatrics in her playful plots from which, in conclusion, she extracts simplified definitions, useful to humanity.

Elysse resides in Waterloo, known as Canada's Technology Triangle and The City of Intelligence—where the Award Winning BlackBerry phones are being designed/manufactured, where science, universities, colleges, arts and financial institutions dominate. Like CANADA itself, a healthy region with a flare for fashion, romance and elegance, perfect atmosphere for creative minds and fantasy prone poets, like Elysse.

ಎಂಡ

Reality vs. Fiction in Elysse's Mind—CANADIAN Poetry

BIBLIOGRAPHY

1. THE MIND OF A POETESS—a true contemporary story
2. I LOVE YOU—CANADIAN Poetry
3. FERTILITY GODDESS SOVATA—inspirational
4. THE BEAUTY OF NATURE—Canadian photography
5. FOREVER LOVED—Lelu, life and death, photographed
6. OPRAH! BEFORE YOU LEAVE ... —novel, satire
7. THE HUNTER OF BEAUTY—CANADA, photography
8. GREAT GLOBAL FUN IN CANADA & USA
    humour (*soon to come*)   **www.elyssepoetis.com**

www.ingramcontent.com/pod-product-compliance
Lightning Source LLC
Chambersburg PA
CBHW070731160426
43192CB00009B/1397